# The Lord's Prayer—
## Equipping Disciples to Live

## Learning how to talk to His Father

## Paul Blackham

With illustrative stories from SASRA Scripture Readers and Area Representatives

**Day**One

© Day One Publications 2017

ISBN 978-1-84625-559-5

British Library Cataloguing in Publication Data available

Joint publication with SASRA and Day One

Day One Publications
Ryelands Road, Leominster, HR6 8NZ, England
Tel 01568 613 740   Fax 01568 611 473
North America  Toll Free 888 329 6630
email  sales@dayone.co.uk
web  www.dayone.co.uk


SASRA
Havelock House, Barrack Road, Aldershot, Hants GU11 3NP
Tel 01252 310033   Fax 03000 302 303
Email  admin@sasra.org.uk
web  www.sasra.org.uk


The image on the cover is used under licence from Shutterstock.com


Printed by TJ International Ltd

# Contents

# Foreword by SASRA's Prayer Coordinator

Like many people 'of a certain age', I can't remember a time when I didn't know the Lord's Prayer. It echoes down the school corridors of time because it was almost certainly as a young child in infant school that I learned it. For many years it was repeated by me and the other pupils of Potternewton Infant School, Leeds, and on into my high-school education, as an end to our daily morning assemblies.

I confess that many years later, when I came to faith and received the Lord as my Saviour, I tended to view the Lord's Prayer as the perfunctory ending to the Communion Service, and for use mostly in corporate gatherings as an acknowledgement of an event which had to have the stamp of approval of the Lord's Prayer at its close.

Then came a day when I saw it in a new light: as a framework onto which I could hang my own personal prayers, a sort of divine mould into which I could pour all my praise, thanksgiving, petitions and heart's desires, which was then turned out onto the altar of His will and purposes, acceptable and pleasing in His sight.

You and I know that prayer must be the priority for any ministry, missionary organization, local church and, of course, for every individual follower of the Lord Jesus Christ. As SASRA Prayer Coordinator, my heart's desire and prayer is that we would all be encouraged, empowered and blessed as we look afresh at the prayer that the Son of Man Himself gave us as our very own family prayer, by which we have the opportunity, with others of the 'household of faith', to join together in addressing 'our

Father'. It is also my prayer that you would be encouraged by the accounts of our Scripture Readers and Area Representatives of how the Lord's Prayer has significantly impacted their ministry to the Armed Forces and changed the lives of so many military personnel.

Maureen McCormack

# Commendations

"**P**aul achieves what few theologians do. He makes the profound simple without falling into the trap of making it simplistic. The book reveals the Tardis nature of The Lord's Prayer. It is more glorious and complex than it looks. What appears to be commonplace is seen to have depth beyond our imagination. The book really does have everything: teaching, pastoral sensitivity, vivid illustration and it's all applied in a relevant manner. It is also dominated by the hero of both the Bible and history, the Lord Jesus Christ. Quite frankly, it's the best small, contemporary book on The Lord's Prayer around."

*David C Meredith, Mission Director, Free Church of Scotland.*

"This warm hearted, well written little book was a pleasure to read and recommend. It did me good! The word of God dwells richly in these pages as each part of The Lord's Prayer is explained using lots of scripture reference and illustration. It is practical and pastoral with real stories from real people bringing the theology of prayer to life. This never becomes merely sentimental. The justice and power of Holy God is clearly portrayed. The privilege of coming before our Father is never underestimated but neither is it doubted because it is made possible in Christ. It was easy to like such a gospel focused approach to prayer."

*Paul Spear, Association of Grace Baptist Churches (SE).*

"This booklet takes the most familiar of words in the Lord's Prayer and yet seems fresh and engaging to read. Each phrase gets a brief but mind stretching chapter which opens our eyes to the scope of the prayer, and reflections from servicemen and women to earth us in every day realities. A wonderful resource for personal devotions. Enjoy it and make the Lord's Prayer a treasure chest for the future too."

*Hugh Palmer, Rector of All Souls Church, Langham Place.*

"'Call upon me and I will answer', says the God of the Bible. True religion is about entering a conversational relationship with God. Everything else is peripheral. The power of Christianity is that, whoever you are, whatever you have done, wherever you are deployed, through Jesus Christ, you can have a living conversational relationship with the true and living God. But what do you say to God? Jesus gave simple instruction in the prayer described in this book. Unpacked with wise advice, humour and relevance, and illustrated with powerful stories of God's work in the lives of military personnel, this book is a profound encouragement to talk to God, to call upon Him and see him answer."

*Mark Grant-Jones has been a Baptist Minister and Army Chaplain with the Royal Army Chaplain's Department. He is currently serving at the NATO Headquarters in Gloucester as the Allied Rapid Reaction Corps Senior Chaplain.*

# 1. Our Father in heaven

One day Jesus was praying in a certain place. When he finished, one of his disciples said to him, 'Lord, teach us to pray, just as John taught his disciples.' He said to them, 'When you pray, say:
"Father,
  hallowed be your name,
  your kingdom come.
  Give us each day our daily bread.
  Forgive us our sins,
    for we also forgive everyone who sins against us.
  And lead us not into temptation"' (Luke 11:1–4).

After this I looked, and there before me was a door standing open in heaven. And the voice I had first heard speaking to me like a trumpet said, 'Come up here, and I will show you what must take place after this.' At once I was in the Spirit, and there before me was a throne in heaven with someone sitting on it. And the one who sat there had the appearance of jasper and ruby. A rainbow that shone like an emerald encircled the throne. Surrounding the throne were twenty-four other thrones, and seated on them were twenty-four elders. They were dressed in white and had crowns of gold on their heads. From the throne came flashes of lightning, rumblings and peals of thunder. In front of the throne, seven lamps were blazing. These are the seven spirits of God. Also in front of the throne there was what looked like a sea of glass, clear as crystal (Revelation 4:1–6).

The disciples watched the way Jesus prayed and they asked Him how to do it. They had seen Jesus do many incredible things—raising the dead, walking on water and controlling the weather—but they didn't ask Jesus how to do any of those things. They realized that if they just knew how to pray like Jesus, everything would be all right.

Knowing how to pray like Jesus is the key to life. To talk to our heavenly Father as Jesus did is the key to knowing life and peace. People who throw all their worries onto their Father can experience joy even in the most terrible circumstances. We have a very limited amount of strength in our frail bodies, and it can so easily be taken from us through illness or age. Yet those who are constantly connected to the almighty and eternal Father have limitless strength to face impossible challenges. The whole purpose and meaning of the death and resurrection of Jesus is this: to bring us to His Father; to make it possible for us to pray to God the Father; to establish that crucial connection, that the Son Himself knew, between us and our Father. Prayer is the most impossible thing in the whole world. For messed-up people like us to speak to the most holy Father in the highest level of reality is utterly impossible—but because of Jesus, it *is* possible.

Sometimes people speak as if the purpose of the work of Jesus was to rescue us from an eternity in hell or to forgive us our sins. These are, of course, very important parts of the work of Jesus, but they are not the great purpose. The reason why we need forgiveness is because our sins disconnect us from God. We cannot talk to our Father while we are still lost in the guilt and shame of our sin. Jesus takes away our sin so that we can come to the Father. Similarly, when we have been brought into the fellowship of the Father we are no longer falling into hell. Knowing God the Father through Jesus in the power of the Spirit takes the problem of hell away. Eternal life is knowing God the Father and Jesus, in the fellowship of the Spirit:

> Now this is eternal life: that they know you, the only true God, and Jesus Christ, whom you have sent (John 17:3).

At the centre of eternal life is prayer. Some people say they can't see the point of praying because it feels as if they are just talking to themselves! Yes, without Jesus that is the best it ever is. However, once we are connected to the Father in heaven through Jesus, it is very, very different. Some of us have prayed for many years and don't find it odd. Some of us are quite new to prayer and find it a bit weird. Others of us have prayed for many years and *still* find it a bit odd. Perhaps the reason why it seems strange and even awkward goes deep into the nature of our lives in a messed-up world. Heaven and earth were designed to be directly connected together. The Bible tells us that at the very beginning there was free access between heaven and earth. Do you remember how the Lord Jesus came to walk in the Garden of Eden with Adam and Eve? It was as if we were designed to speak to the Living God more directly, face to face. We were not designed to talk to Him across the division between heaven and earth.

Speaking to an invisible friend does not come naturally to everybody. However, spending a lot of time talking to an invisible friend has actually never been more common. When I lived in Central London I used to see people chatting away to invisible friends all the time. I could look out of my kitchen window and see dozens of people every day walking along talking with great passion to their invisible friends. The fact that they had earpieces in their ear and were talking on mobile phones led them to believe that the invisible friends they were speaking to genuinely existed, but it still struck me as very strange: they were connected to their invisible friends in a way I was not. They were linked to them and knew their voice.

That is the whole thing with prayer as well. Until we have a genuine connection to the Almighty Father in heaven, the whole thing might sound a little unbelievable and strange. We just cannot pray if we do not have a living connection to the Living God. We just won't believe that it is real unless we are actually connected to the person on the other end of the telephone. Given that Jesus was frequently on the telephone line to God the Father, it made a great deal of sense to talk to Him about the best way to pray. We must never forget that Jesus is Lord: He is the Lord God of Israel. He did not begin His work or existence when He was conceived in the Virgin Mary. He is the eternal Son of the Father, fully equal with His Father and the Spirit in the life of God. The Father created all things *in*, *through* and *for* His eternal Son, the Lord Jesus. The Father did not suddenly need a mediator two thousand years ago! Jesus has always been the Mediator between God and the world. For thousands of years before He was born of Mary, God the Son gave His ancient people access to the Father. It is helpful to remember that, when the disciples asked Jesus how to pray, the Lord Jesus had already listened to millions and millions of prayers in the highest heaven for long ages before He was born as one of us.

Let's begin with our *need* to talk to our Father in heaven. If we don't pray it is because we think we don't have to or don't need to. I once heard a story about a military man whose wife was pregnant. Her waters suddenly broke and the baby was coming: it was all happening so fast. He rang the midwife, who said that because the baby was actually coming out there was no way they could get to a hospital and neither could she get to them in time. She stayed on the phone while the man logged onto YouTube and watched a video called 'How to Deliver a Baby in a Taxi'. It all went relatively well and he was interviewed on TV and radio throughout the following week. He made the point that his training in the navy made him realize how important getting expert help is in any crisis situation. He needed to reach out to get some support and help in a difficult situation. The same is true for us. If we believe that life is easy, that we can just relax and enjoy ourselves, that we are in a completely safe environment, then we are not really going to seek serious expert help and support. If, on the other hand, we see that life is a crisis situation, a land of exile far removed from the Living God, a passing darkness where the powers of evil are ruling, a dangerous environment where we can so easily be drawn away into worthless rubbish and a lost eternity—*then* we realize that we desperately need expert help and a very strong dose of daily support.

> Is prayer your steering wheel or your spare tyre?
> (Corrie Ten Boom).

We call out to heaven, not because it is a 'religious duty', but because it is a basic necessity of real life. Jesus begins by calling on 'Our Father *in heaven*'. So, what is this heaven? *What is heaven?* What does it mean that our Father is in heaven? The Bible tells us that there are 'three heavens' and that the Father lives in the third heaven. The first heaven is the place where birds fly around and clouds float. The second heaven is space, the place where *Star Trek* takes place. The third heaven is beyond all that.

Imagine standing on a mountain top sensing the huge open space around you. Appreciate the birds and clouds that move about in this first heaven. We live and move within this heaven. We can be awestruck by its size and glory. When we are standing on a hill or mountain, this first heaven can seem huge. If we see a storm raging, with lightning and rain, it can feel overwhelming and frightening. Notice how the birds fly around within this first heaven, singing to one another. They greet the sunrise each day with song and gaze down on the events on the earth from the heights as they fly. Remember the clouds that drift gently through the first heaven.

Now imagine that you are moving up and out into space, with all the special effects, and you are moving out through the first heaven and going into the second. Imagine that you are moving up above the clouds and climbing still higher into orbit around the earth. Can you imagine the Planet Earth below you? Now you are moving out across the solar system and you can see Planet Earth getting smaller, with the sun in the distance. The planets of our solar system pass by as you move out further into this second heaven. Imagine that you are picking up speed and the sun and the earth become mixed in with other star systems as you move out across the Milky Way. You have probably seen many pictures of space: distant stars, galaxies and big clouds of purple and blue gas. The clouds that floated around in the first heaven seem so small and feeble now compared with these much greater clouds of the second heaven. Consider the difference in size and power between the first heaven and the second heaven.

Now imagine that you are travelling beyond the Milky Way galaxy. You see other galaxies and yet you still travel on. The countless galaxies are bewildering in their variety and size; and yet, can you imagine moving even beyond this second heaven into the third heaven? Can you imagine that you could, in some strange way, move up into a higher level of reality? Can you imagine moving up into another heaven above and beyond all of space as we know it? Remember how small the first heaven seemed when you were thinking of all the galaxies and stars. Just as the earth looked small from the stars, so the whole of the universe of stars looks small as you begin to move into the third heaven, the highest heaven. Imagine a level of reality that is as far beyond the galaxies as the galaxies are beyond our clouds and birds. In this highest heaven there are clouds of glory and winged creatures that fly around, and these seem so wonderful that we just can't describe them any more. In the Bible, whenever people try to describe this level of reality they are lost for words. We can hardly make sense of what they say. Consider Ezekiel's vision in chapter 1 of his book, or Daniel's glimpse in chapter 7 of his book. The hundreds of millions of angels that fly around in this highest heaven seem so glorious that even the greatest Christians of the Bible may mistakenly worship them (Revelation 19:10)! As you look up, you see what seems to be a celestial rainbow, and within that rainbow is a throne so wonderful and glorious that the entire universe is nothing compared with that throne. On this throne sits 'Someone' and at His side is Jesus, the glorious Son of Man, who looks like a Lamb that has been slaughtered. Surrounding the throne is the sevenfold Holy Spirit in all His power and depth. Around these Three, around the Father, Son and Holy Spirit, you sense millions of creatures. This highest heaven is filled not only with the great angelic host, but also with all the millions of saints who have trusted in Jesus since the world began. They too are caught up into the glorious life of the third heaven, resting and waiting for that great day of justice and resurrection.

*That* is heaven and the Living God to whom we talk in prayer. *That* is the kind of scale and wonder that must be in our minds as we think about God: the Father, Son and Holy Spirit. In fact, whenever we pray or praise, it is *that* Father in heaven who needs to be always in our minds. Whatever we pray for is so easily done from the perspective of the third heaven. When we think about the size, power and glory of the third heaven, and the Father's throne at the centre of everything, all our problems seem so very small. We might be praying about an argument over a parking space at work or a boundary fence at home, yet how different these matters seem when we are seated with Jesus in the third heaven speaking to the glorious Father! Many things we thought were worth bothering about simply fade away into insignificance when we are caught up in the worship and life of the third heaven. What are all the empires of the world when viewed from that throne room? All our problems and fears, and the whole of our brief life, seem so different when we view them from the throne of the Father at the centre of the third heaven.

This is why we begin with the statement 'Our Father in heaven'. Everything looks different when we think of our Father at the centre of the third heaven surrounded by hundreds of millions of angelic creatures and God's triumphant people of past ages filled with the glory of heaven. Let's daily begin our prayers with this deep sense of our holy Father who invites us into the third heaven to sit with Him and sort out the issues of our lives and the world.

# Reflections

## ASR Lee McDade

For a Scripture Reader the gift of prayer, personal and public, is one of the most important tools in the toolbox. Our personal prayer life is a vital part of our work: we should always speak to God, our heavenly Father, before speaking to others. And to be able to offer to pray for someone is an incredible privilege. I have never had prayer refused!

I was on my way out of a camp in Germany one night. It had been a spiritually dry night so I had decided to go home. On most camps you have to sign out at the guardroom after a certain time, which is what I was doing when I was asked if I could talk with one of two detained soldiers. I said I would, and I had a nice chat with the chap. At the end I offered to pray for him. On hearing the word 'prayer' the other detained soldier came in and asked me to pray for him as well. As we were about to begin, the guard commander came in looking concerned and asked what I was doing. I told him I was about to pray for the two soldiers! I thought he was going to ask me to leave but he didn't: he sat down and asked me to pray for him as well because he had just found out he was being made redundant. What had begun as a dry evening became a wonderful time of prayer and witness!

I love praying for people and with people; it is such a privilege. 'Thank you, Lord, for the gift of prayer.

Thank you that we can call you Father and that you are a Father who is concerned for His children.'

Over the last two years especially, I have had the privilege of working with some fine young men who are still willing to join the British Army and are willing to put their lives on the line for Queen, Country and Freedom. As you can imagine, these young men come to us from all sorts of different backgrounds, and many have had no father figure in their lives or have suffered at the hands of their dads. Some of the stories I have been told are tragic, but it has been my honour to share with many of these young men about my relationship with my heavenly Father, a Father who cares for His children, a Father who is loyal, a Father who can forgive and assist with forgiving others, a Father with whom we can have constant communication, and a Father who desires to have a relationship with us. It reminds me of the privilege I have in being able to call our holy God 'Abba', to have that relationship with our Father through His Son, Jesus. As you can imagine, for some I meet this seems too good to be true; but my prayer is that some will be adopted by the same heavenly Father who has adopted me, the Father who has, and always will be, with me, who holds me in His hands, who knows me inside out.

## ASR & Area Rep Paul Somerville

When I met Mark in his barracks room I noticed a photo of a uniformed soldier on his beside locker. I asked if it was his brother, but he replied that it was his best friend. With tears in his eyes he shared that they had both joined the army together, passed out together, arrived at the same battalion together and did everything together: 'We were good mates, inseparable. We deployed together to Iraq, and on one patrol, as we dismounted from our armoured Land Rover, a shot rang out and I saw my best friend fall to the ground. I watched as his life's blood seeped into the ground. He died, I lived, and I'm struggling to cope with it all.' I encouraged him to have a chat with the battalion Padre who would, among other things, be able to advise him of the available support. I then took the opportunity to share how God the Father witnessed the death of His Son, Jesus, at the hands of Roman soldiers, and yet it is through Jesus' death that we can be reconciled to God the Father, and then through Christ He becomes God *our* Father.

## ASR Roddy MacLeod

In my ministry I often engage and meet with people who show an interest in knowing more about the Christian faith. I often start off with a group of ten or a dozen who are interested to learn what the Christian faith is all about. My main objective is to lead them to a point where God actually becomes their Father. As the weeks go by we look at the fall of man into sin and the solution of Christ on the cross. For many in the group, talk of a new birth, a changed heart and life, and a God who is real is all a bit extreme and some do not finish the course. Among those who stay until the end of the course—and I am thinking of two particular young men recently—some understand that God is their Father: the light in their eyes and the sheer joy on their faces and in their hearts is incredible. For these two men I mentioned, it was obvious to me that they had been saved and were now enjoying the reality of a relationship with the living and true God.

## ASR William Wade

Many soldiers who join the army do so from fairly broken homes. One such soldier is Aldo, currently serving with 16 Air Assault Brigade, Colchester. I first met Aldo in Germany around 2004 when he arrived one night at our SASRA Soldiers' Fellowship which met in our home. He shared with us that he had been orphaned as a child in Malawi, but had made it across to the UK and joined the British Army as a Commonwealth soldier. When he came to our home, he knew little of Christianity, but seemed happy to be with us as we discussed the Bible and prayed together.

One evening at the fellowship, having been coming for around two months, Aldo called me aside just as others were arriving and settling in for the meeting. He told me that not only did he feel the need to commit his life to Jesus, but that he wanted to do it right there and then. So in the kitchen of our little

SASRA home on the army base in Rheindahlen, Germany, Aldo prayed to God and trusted in Jesus' work on the cross for his own salvation. It was the greatest of starts to our fellowship that night! What was really special over the coming weeks and months was that Aldo was now able to pray to his heavenly Father, having not known who his earthly father was. He was now an adopted son of the greatest Dad anyone could ever have: the Eternal Father of Scripture! What a blessing it is to be able to pray, 'Our Father.'

# 2. **Our Father**

J esus prayed for His disciples and for all of us who would believe in Him through the preaching of those apostles:

> My prayer is not for them alone. I pray also for those who will believe in me through their message, that all of them may be one, Father, just as you are in me and I am in you. May they also be in us so that the world may believe that you have sent me. I have given them the glory that you gave me, that they may be one as we are one—I in them and you in me—so that they may be brought to complete unity. Then the world will know that you sent me and have loved them even as you have loved me.

> Father, I want those you have given me to be with me where I am, and to see my glory, the glory you have given me because you loved me before the creation of the world.

> Righteous Father, though the world does not know you, I know you, and they know that you have sent me. I have made you known to them, and will continue to make you known in order that the love you have for me may be in them and that I myself may be in them (John 17:20–26).

We cannot leave things with us standing in the vast and intimidating wonders of the third heaven. We have to go back to the truth of 'our Father'. It is such a wonderful beginning. *Our Father*. Think again *who* is teaching us to say that. Jesus has that relationship with His Eternal Father. He has always been with His Father, for everlasting ages before there was a universe. The eternal identity of Jesus is the beloved Son of the Father. He has revelled in the infinite love and trust of His Father for endless ages and is utterly sure of that love and trust for endless ages to come. In return He utterly trusts His Father and is always eager to hear His will and obey Him in the power of the Spirit. What a glorious eternal family of love and trust!

What was His reaction to the fact that the Father wanted to bring in a large number of other children alongside Him? Perhaps at first Jesus might have been happy about that, so long as those children were extremely well behaved and came from a very good family and social background. But 'No', said the Father, 'I want to bring in the most difficult kind of children: children who come from a broken and messed-up world—a world that is at war with everything we stand for. Children who will refuse to live according to our life, children who will require unbelievably large amounts of love, support, help and encouragement. In fact, even to be able to bring them in, you will have to give your own life, Jesus, for them. And, at the end of it all, I want to love them just as I have loved you, treat them just as I have treated you and give them everything that I had for you.' When confronted with this extremely demanding plan, Jesus said: 'Here I am, send me. It's a wonderful idea! Let's make it happen. What can I do to help?'

> You were dead in your transgressions and sins, in which you used to live when you followed the ways of this world and of the ruler of the kingdom of the air, the spirit who is now at work in those who are disobedient. All of us also lived among them at one time, gratifying the cravings of our flesh and following its desires and

thoughts. Like the rest, we were by nature deserving of wrath. But because of his great love for us, God, who is rich in mercy, made us alive with Christ even when we were dead in transgressions—it is by grace you have been saved. And God raised us up with Christ and seated us with him in the heavenly realms in Christ Jesus (Ephesians 2:1–6).

In Matthew 6, Jesus has come into the far country to bring the wild children into the Father's household, and they have heard how He speaks to His Father. They want to do the same. They want to talk to the Father just as the Eternal Son talks to Him. If we remember Jesus' story of the prodigal son, the wild and broken son, we know how very far from the Father's house the son had strayed. Not only did he wish the Father was dead when he asked for his inheritance early, but he wasted all that treasure in the worst possible ways, in sinful and shameful living. That wicked son ended up working for pagans, feeding unclean animals and eating pig slop. In the story Jesus told, the older brother represented the religious people of Israel who wanted nothing to do with that worthless brother.

Before Jesus told the story of this wasteful, lost son, He had told two other stories about searching for lost things. He first told the story of a shepherd who went out to search for a lost sheep. Then He described how a woman turned her house upside down to look for a lost coin. In this final story the father seems to be searching the horizon for the return of his lost son. However, what actually happened is that Jesus the Eternal Son came into the far country to find the lost sons and daughters, to pick them up, wash them and carry them home to the Father's house.

When these wild children heard how the eternally loved and faithful Son spoke to His Father, they wanted to share in that same love. They wanted to speak to the Father just as if they had never strayed, never been lost, never let the Father down. How would the older, natural brother relate to all these adopted children who wanted to be like Him? Would He remind them how they were not *really* children, that they shouldn't try to get too close to *His* Father? No. Jesus immediately wants us to begin our prayers with these two wonderful words: *Our Father*. Jesus immediately includes us alongside Himself as brothers and sisters of His Eternal Father. He wants us to talk to the Father as if we had the same relationship with the Father that He does.

The word 'our' is perhaps the most precious word in the whole of the Lord's Prayer, because it guarantees that we speak to the Father through the Lord Jesus Himself. We speak to the Father because Jesus shares His life with everyone who trusts Him. Jesus puts His arms around our shoulders and says 'our Father', including us with Himself. We are not speaking to a majestic king who likes to keep people at arm's length. No, we are speaking to a loving, safe, trustworthy father. For some people who have never had any experience of a safe, loving father, the first two words of Jesus' pattern of prayer may be as far as they get for some time. Some are quite quickly thrilled to find the father they always should have had, but others find that it takes much longer to learn the trust, love and safety of this Eternal Father.

Some of us know a lot about that journey. To know that we have a constant open invitation to sit with our Eternal Father, in complete safety, surrounded by His love, care, wisdom and support—this is the rock-solid foundation of life and prayer. This is the starting point to which Jesus' death, resurrection and ascension get us. We come to our heavenly Father, to the Person who knows everything about us and still loves us and accepts us. He knows what we need from Him before ever we open our mouths to ask Him. He is more generous and indulgent than any earthly, temporary father. Jesus Himself tells us that the Father loves us just as the Father loved Jesus before the world began.

> I pray also for those who will believe in me through their [his disciples'] message, that all of them may be one, Father, just as you are in me and I am in you. May they also be in us so that the world may believe that you have sent me. I have given them the glory that you gave me, that they may be one as we are one—I in them and you in me—so that they may be brought to complete unity. Then the world will know that you sent me and have loved them even as you have loved me.

> Father, I want those you have given me to be with me where I am, and to see my glory, the glory you have given me because you loved me before the creation of the world (John 17:20–24).

This wonderful heavenly Father always has time for us and will always respond to our prayers. Whether He deals with them in quite the way we ask or not is something else, but He is always there for us, no matter what other pressures face Him.

> Some people think God does not like to be troubled with our constant asking. The way to trouble God is not to ask at all (Dwight L. Moody).

*This* is the Father who will never walk out on us or abandon us. *This* is the Father who is utterly committed to us for ever and ever through life, through death, and on into an everlasting future. *This* is the One who is at the very centre of all reality, sitting on the throne of the third heaven; the Father who gathers us in Jesus and by the power of His Spirit brings us to sit with Him on that throne so that we can cast all our worries and troubles onto Him. You weren't designed to live without talking to God, so this very day start living life as it was meant to be, genuinely talking to the Father in the highest heaven every single day.

# Reflections

## ASR Gavin Dickson

In my role as a Scripture Reader I meet many people who not only don't believe in God but are even actively against the idea of there being a God. Often the conversation reaches strange avenues as they are more inclined to believe in aliens than in God! Sometimes, though, the conversations turn to prayer after an introduction to the gospel. I find myself explaining that if what we have talked about has stirred something in them, instead of telling me, they should pray to God, alone, in a quiet place, and ask this God we have been talking about if He is real and if this Jesus did die to save them.

After a long chat with one soldier about life, God and the Bible, I found that I had hit a block and nothing more I could say would convince him of his need to be saved. I ended the conversation by asking him if what we had talked about had caused him to think, and I challenged him to go home that night and pray. I believe that prayer changes people, and I see evidence of this in my ministry.

I also talked to a group of soldiers' wives about heaven, following a discussion of the Christmas film *It's a Wonderful Life*. Their ideas on where heaven is and what happens there were varied, fanciful and unbiblical. I was able to share with them what the Bible says about heaven, and about God's justice and promise of peace in His kingdom. It was a privilege to tell them of the reality of heaven.

### ASR Ray Hendricks

While visiting the detention centre just after lunch one day and finding it empty, I struck up a conversation with the Cpl guard commander, Cpl 'W', who had served approximately eighteen years and was in his late thirties. He seemed to believe in a higher power, but beyond that he did not much care. Cpl 'W' had two children, one a toddler and the other about eleven years old. I asked him to describe the love he had for his children and how it was different from other types of love. Cpl 'W' spoke of the intensity of his love for his children and how he would do anything for them, even protect them with his life. I shared with him how God is *our* Father, for He created us, as explained in Genesis 1:26. I shared how that deep love for our children is a fraction of the love that our Father God has for His. I shared with him how God's love for us caused Him to send His only Son Jesus Christ (having God's Spirit in Him and being perfectly sinless) to die for all mankind. I pray that, even though he heard only the basic message, he will start to have a change of heart towards the gospel and Jesus Christ.

## ASR Nick Wilson

A soldier had just bought a lovely mirror in a pub with a poem on it. 'Do you know this lovely poem?' he asked me. It was Psalm 23! I explained to him the essential importance of knowing God and Jesus personally and I left him with a Bible to read. I went back to see him several weeks later. 'I have been reading the Bible and I do not think I am saved; I do not know God as my Father or my Shepherd. How do I become a Christian?' I showed him what the Bible says about salvation. We both knelt down in his room as he accepted Christ as his personal Saviour. He marvelled at the reality of calling God his Father!

## ASR Tiaan De Klerk

We, as believers in the Lord Jesus, through Jesus' sacrifice upon the cross, His righteous life as a man, His conquering of death and His completed work, may now call the Creator 'our Father'. It is truly amazing! This beautiful truth jolts a memory of a conversation I had one morning in Prince Phillip Barracks with Darrel (not his real name), a young nineteen-year-old British soldier who had been serving in the army for just under two years and was close to the end of his second-phase training. This time was not unlike other times, but his story stood out. I asked him about his family life and it became clear that he was uncomfortable replying. Darrel said that he wanted to speak about his past but found it difficult. He told me that he found the idea of a sovereign, loving God hard to believe because of the pain in his life. He explained that he had three younger siblings; growing up, their home was frequently visited by unknown men. None of them were ever around long enough to be known and at those times he was pretty much ignored. The most painful experience Darrel spoke of was his mother's anger. When anger got the better of her and she wanted to punish him, she would run the bath and stick his head under the water for several seconds. He said he was now working with social services, hoping to gain custody of his two younger siblings who were still at home.

Many soldiers come from difficult and broken families. My heart cried out for this young man, and my only desire is that he would come to Christ and truly have a Father who loves him. How many children grow up in households like this and never hear of 'our Father'! We so often read over phrases in the Bible, not stopping in awe at the wonder of what is being said. We can call God 'our Father in heaven'! What a privilege, what an honour, what a glorious God we serve! Oh, that all may come to know Him as our Father through the Lord Jesus, the Christ! That Darrel might come to know his Father in heaven! For truly His Son is worth the price of His labour.

## ASR Meg Atkinson

It was about 3.15 a.m. on Christmas Day morning and I was walking into a hangar where aircraft were being repaired. 'Meg, what are you doing here?' exclaimed a member of staff. 'I could ask you the same,' I replied. 'We have to be here on our shift, but you don't, Meg.'

Looking up to the heavens, I replied: 'My boss is 24/7, 365 days a year. Of course, I am but a mere mortal, so can't compete and need my sleep.' However, it being the day chosen to celebrate the Lord's birth gave me a great opportunity to share Scripture and seasonal chocolate. Working 'out of hours' shows in a small measure the greater love our Father in heaven has for His creation.

# 3. Hallowed be Your name

Way back in Isaiah chapter 6, the prophet Isaiah saw and heard the seraphim when the Lord God visited the temple around 750 BC.

> In the year that King Uzziah died, I saw the Lord, high and exalted, seated on a throne; and the train of his robe filled the temple. Above him were seraphim, each with six wings: with two wings they covered their faces, with two they covered their feet, and with two they were flying. And they were calling to one another:
>
> 'Holy, holy, holy is the LORD Almighty;
>   the whole earth is full of his glory.'
>
> At the sound of their voices the doorposts and thresholds shook and the temple was filled with smoke.
>
> 'Woe to me!' I cried. 'I am ruined! For I am a man of unclean lips, and I live among a people of unclean lips, and my eyes have seen the King, the LORD Almighty' (Isaiah 6:1–5).

Those angels cried out *to one another*, 'Holy, holy, holy is the LORD Almighty; the whole earth is full of his glory.' They were shouting this truth *to one another* as if they constantly needed to be reminded of it, as if they dared not let this truth slip from their minds even for a moment. More than 750 years after Isaiah, John was allowed to see into the very heart of the third heaven, right to the very centre of all reality, and he saw and heard the angels still proclaiming the very same words, the very same message:

> In the centre, round the throne, were four living creatures, and they were covered with eyes, in front

and behind. The first living creature was like a lion, the second was like an ox, the third had a face like a man, the fourth was like a flying eagle. Each of the four living creatures had six wings and was covered with eyes all around, even under its wings. Day and night they never stop saying:

'Holy, holy, holy
is the Lord God Almighty,
who was, and is, and is to come' (Revelation 4:6–8).

For 750 years those angels had been declaring that truth to one another, making sure that the third heaven was full of that truth: the Lord God Almighty is *holy*. In that highest level of reality, in the control centre of existence, there is constant, never-ending angelic worship, and the first and central theme of that worship is this:

Holy, holy, holy
is the Lord God Almighty.

That is how important the holiness of God really is, and this is why the Lord Jesus told us always to begin our prayers with this truth: Holy, holy, holy is the Lord God Almighty. At the beginning of our daily prayers we are to echo on earth what is constantly declared in heaven. The Name of the Father is seen as holy in the highest heaven, so we ask that we too might know that reality. We want to give the respect and honour due to the Father. *We pray that we would relate to the Father in the right way.*

The problem is that we always tend to bring God down to our own level. We tend to drift into thinking of Him as tame and safe. It's understandable to want to think of God like that; it is much more comfortable to invent a god who fits into our life, our feelings, our desires and our ideals.

Many people tell me how they like to imagine God and it is nearly always as something or someone very safe and very tame, a 'spiritual' warm blanket of love and safety. The critics of Christianity see this quite clearly when they point out how many religious people simply project their own hopes and dreams into the heavens to make a god who makes them feel better. Of course we want to think of God in a way that makes us feel good, in a way that we can handle, *but it isn't true*. God is not tame, but dangerous. He is not random or bad tempered, *but* He is not tame. He is a consuming fire, and none of us can survive in His presence.

One preacher puts it like this:

> God is completely different, dangerous, alien, holy, wild. When God shows up in Scripture, people cower and tremble. They go mute. The ones who manage speech fall into despair. People constantly faint with terror when they get near to Him. Take the prophet Daniel. He could stare down lions, but when the heavens opened, he passed out.[1]

In the Lord's Prayer, Jesus is telling us that *we need to remember who God is* before we say anything else. The kind of god our messed-up human minds *invent* is not like the true Living God, and every single day we need to come back to our *real* heavenly Father who is holy. When we ask 'Hallowed be Your name', we are asking something like this: 'Show us that You are more than we ever think or imagine; show us what You are really like; show us

---

1 Drew Dyck, 'How We Forgot the Holiness of God', *Christianity Today*, 20 May 2014.

how different, separate, pure and dedicated You really are. Make sure that we give You the credit You really deserve.'

So what does the word 'holy' mean? Thomas Watson said: 'Holiness is the most sparkling jewel of God's crown; it is the name by which God is known.'[2] God is the Holy One.

There are three aspects to the word 'holy': *different*, *separate* and *focused*. Let's think about each of these aspects of the Father's holiness so that we might understand why *this* is the very first request in the Lord's Prayer.

## DIFFERENT

That the Father is *holy* means that the Father is *different*. The primary meaning of holy is 'divide': it comes from an ancient word that meant 'to cut' or 'to divide'. To be holy is to be different. Which sin is most condemned in the whole Bible? Greed? Sexual immorality? Stealing? Violence? No, it is *idolatry*. Idolatry is when we make a god for ourselves, when we worship something we have made or imagined. *Idolatry is worshipping what I want to worship.* People often say something like this: 'I couldn't believe in a god who ...', and then they describe something they don't like about the Bible, Jesus, or God as they understand Him to be. 'I couldn't believe in a god who judges our sexual behaviour ... I couldn't believe in a god who suffers or has a broken heart ... I couldn't believe in a god who sends people to hell ... I couldn't believe in a god who allows suffering ... I couldn't believe in a god who lets evil people get away with what they have done ... I couldn't believe

2  Thomas Watson, *A Body of Divinity* (Edinburgh: Banner of Truth, 1984), p. 91.

in a god who became human … I couldn't believe in a god who will judge the world … I couldn't believe in a god who has written such violent things in the Bible … I couldn't believe in a god who is invisible.'

It is all too easy to think of *a god who is like us*, who is caught up in the same kind of thinking and feelings *we* have. Other people go to the opposite extreme and just imagine a god who is the opposite of all our human weaknesses, a god who is so far away that he/she/it has nothing to do with us, a god who is too high ever to deal directly with us, a god who wants to keep us at arm's length, a god who is too far away to make any real difference. Whether we make a god who is just like us or a god who is the opposite of us, these gods are all defined by *us*. We need to be serious about this. Just because we invent a god who is all-powerful and distant doesn't mean that our god is more real than the weak and cosy god invented by others. The abstract gods of religious philosophy are just as false as the cosy gods of popular spirituality. Whether we imagine God to be just like us or simply the opposite of us, we pull Him down to our level and we don't take Him seriously. In Isaiah 29:16 God says: 'You turn things upside down, as if the potter were thought to be like the clay!'

It is good to appreciate the context of this powerful accusation. The Lord God confronts His people to tell them that they have allowed their minds and their lives to be controlled by merely human rules and human intelligence. Their religion might make perfect common sense to *them*, but it is offensive and foolish in the courts of heaven. The deep problem is that when we limit the Living God to the size of our intelligence, we think that we can hide our plans from Him.

The Lord says:

'These people come near to me with their mouth
  and honour me with their lips,
  but their hearts are far from me.
Their worship of me
  is made on merely human rules they have been
taught.
Therefore once more I will astound these people
  with wonder upon wonder;
the wisdom of the wise will perish,
  the intelligence of the intelligent will vanish.'
*Woe to those who go to great depths*
  *to hide their plans from the LORD,*
*who do their work in darkness and think,*
  *'Who sees us? Who will know?'*
You turn things upside down,
  as if the potter were thought to be like the clay!
Shall what is formed say to the one who formed it,
'You did not make me'?
Can the pot say to the potter,
'You know nothing'? (Isaiah 29:13–16, emphasis
added).

God explains that, when we think of Him as being just like us, we don't take Him seriously and we think that we can hide from Him or that He doesn't really notice what we are doing. Psalm 50:18–22 takes up the same theme. When we think of God as being the same as us, we end up doing what is evil:

If you see a thief, you are pleased with him,
  and you keep company with adulterers.
You give your mouth free rein for evil,

and your tongue frames deceit.
You sit and speak against your brother;
  you slander your own mother's son.
These things you have done, and I have been silent;
  you thought that I was one like yourself.
But now I rebuke you and lay the charge before you.
Mark this, then, you who forget God,
  lest I tear you apart, and there be none to deliver!
(ESV)

When I was a young teenager I once told a friend how I liked to imagine God and why I struggled with some of the things the Bible said about Him. This friend said to me, 'It doesn't matter what *you* think about God; the only question is, what is God *really* like?' We need to deal with the God who is actually there. Yes, the Father is enthroned in the highest heaven, far above and beyond the mess of this world; yet this Father actually numbers the very hairs on our heads and sent His own Son to find us, no matter how lost we are. This real Father in heaven is not like any of the gods human beings imagine. He is *different*. He is higher, greater and more terrifying than we could ever imagine—*but* He is also more loving and kind, more generous and more patient than we could ever imagine. He is different. How do we hallow the Father's Name? The gods that are like us, the gods we imagine, are always cruel and oppressive *in the end*. For example, we might want a beautiful god, a god of beauty. But this sort of god demands that we too are beautiful, so we live a constant battle trying to become the beautiful idol we think we should be. We might want a perfectionist god who won't have anything to do with anything that is imperfect, but when we worship our obsession with perfection we create a god who can never be satisfied, a god who makes our life a misery as we are always trying to be good enough. It is very good news that the Father is holy: He is different. He is not like us. He was not invented by *us* and He needs nothing from us. He is what He is.

## SEPARATE

That the Father is *holy* means that He is *separate*. Often when we begin our prayers we are caught up in the mess of our lives and the world. Perhaps we feel dirty and ashamed because of what we have done, thought or said, or because of what has been done *to* us. Perhaps it is the mess of the world around us that feels overwhelming. It can feel as if the world is a flood of darkness and evil. We come to pray about all the things that are bothering us in life: the situations we are in seem hopeless, and we can't see a way to escape. The wonderful truth is that our Father in heaven is *separate. He is not part of the mess.* The Bible describes God as *a firm place to stand* in the swamps of life. He is separate; and when we come to Him in prayer, we come to the One who is set apart from the trouble. We are so caught up in the troubles of the here and now that we can't see what is going on. But the Father is *separate.* He can see what is *really* happening, what is coming in the future, and where we are going.

Have you ever been in a big maze at a castle or theme park? They are surprisingly difficult to deal with because we quickly lose our sense of direction and we can keep going round and round the same dead ends. Most of these mazes have an attendant sitting high up above the maze who can see where we are and how we can get out. The attendant will shout down instructions to us if we are lost, leading us out of the maze to safety. That is a bit like the holiness of the Father. He is separate from the mess and the problems, able to help us from a position of power and stability. He is pure—untouched by the lies, hypocrisy, selfishness and evil of this world. When we come to our heavenly Father, we are turning to purity away from all the impurity that is in us and around us.

Think about this: the Father is so holy that when He sent His Son, Jesus, into the world, Jesus could live among us, *as one of us*, and yet never sin. He was undefiled by the sin and pollution around Him. When He touched lepers, the pollution did not infect *Him*; rather His cleanness was passed on to the lepers and they were made clean. When He touched a dead body, the pollution of death could not get Him; rather the dead body sprang to life again. If we want to see how separate from our mess and sin the Father really is, we must look carefully at Jesus of Nazareth. If we are sinking down in a swamp or in quicksand, we need somebody who is *separate* from the swamp or quicksand. We need help from solid ground—help from somebody who is on the rock.

*Our Father in heaven is not part of the problem: He is the solution. He is the solid rock in the quicksands of life. He wants us to run to Him as the one solid place in a world that is falling apart.*

## FOCUSED

That the Father is *holy* means that He is *focused*. He never gets tired. He never sleeps. He never gets distracted. In the Bible we see that things were holy if they were dedicated to just *one special use* in the temple: the clothes of the priests were holy because they were only to be used in the temple. The priest didn't wear those holy robes when he was sitting around at home or doing the washing up. Those robes were holy because they were dedicated to just one purpose. To be holy means to be single-minded, focused, dedicated. The Father never slumbers or sleeps. He is never distracted by any other business. He is never checking social media or emails when He is 'listening' to us. His whole attention is always given completely to this business of ruling and redeeming the world through Jesus. The Father is always focused on building up his people around Jesus by the Spirit. He is never 'off duty'. He has no 'private life'. There are no skeletons in the cupboard. He has only one purpose for you and for everybody: that we become just like Jesus by the power of His Spirit. In other words, the Father is utterly reliable. The holiness of the Father means the reliability of the Father. We can depend on Him totally, and *that* is why we can pray to Him, casting all our anxieties upon Him.

The Father is *holy*, and that means that He is *different*, *separate* and *focused*. How, then, do we hallow the Father's Name? What happens when we know that He is different, separate, pure and focused? *We trust Him*. We know that we are hallowing the Name of the Father *if* we trust Him completely and do what He tells us. In Numbers 20 Moses did not trust the Lord; Moses did not do what he was told to do. The Lord confronted Moses with these words: '*Because you did not trust in me enough to honour me as holy* in the sight of the Israelites, you will not bring this community into the land I give them' (Numbers 20:12).

The Father is holy—and therefore He is utterly trustworthy. Whatever He says we must treat as utterly true and reliable. When we act as if His words are unreliable, *then* we treat Him as unholy. Every day we need to begin by honouring our heavenly Father as holy. Every day we must begin by trusting Him. Every day we must say 'no' to the lies of the world, the flesh and the devil, and 'yes' to our heavenly Father. Everything that comes in the rest of the Lord's Prayer depends on *that*.

# Reflections

## ASR Roddy MacLeod

I was anxious to teach two men who had accepted God as their Father through Christ that to 'hallow' God's name means to live in the light of His holy Word, the Bible. We met when their programme allowed and talked about all sorts of things, but my main emphasis was to point them to the Scriptures and its authority, explaining that 'hallowing' God's Name means honouring and obeying our Father. The two of them were like sponges soaking up the Word of God. The main reason I wanted to make sure they would rely wholly on the Bible was because many would tell them otherwise. It was a joy and a privilege to have this time, and it was with great concern of heart that I saw them leave Pirbright; but I trust they are equipped to continue growing in their faith, keeping God's Name holy, through the Word of God.

## ASR Tiaan De Klerk

As believers we must have a foundational view and understanding of God as infinitely holy! Isaiah 6:3 tells us about the seraphim calling to one another that the Lord is 'Holy, holy, holy' and that the 'earth is full of his glory'. In the Westminster Shorter Catechism we read that God is a Spirit, infinite, eternal and unchangeable, in His being, wisdom, power, holiness, justice, goodness and truth. What a glorious God we serve! We must desire to see God's Name considered and treated as holy all over the earth (Psalm 96:9). We must desire to be holy out of obedience to the One who loves us (1 Peter 1:15–16).

Working among soldiers who daily blaspheme against our holy God, among soldiers who delight in sexual immorality, it is easy to lose focus and feel despair. Many of these young men do not even want to dwell on the question of whether or not there is a God. They find themselves oblivious to the need of a Saviour. Their conscience convicts them of sin, but they suppress it.

One day I had a chance meeting with a group of four Commonwealth soldiers I knew from previous encounters. When they were posted in Bordon they used to come for Bible studies and seemed to be acting in accordance with God's will. I sat down to chat with them and inquire how they were doing in their walk with God. They were all very positive, saying that things were great and God had been faithful. It didn't take long, though, before they started blaspheming and swearing. They had been drawn in by the ways of the world and they did not consider God's holiness. I opened the Bible to share with them that as Christians we are set apart, not walking in the ways of the world, but rather drawing near to God that we may reflect His glory in some small way. They did not seem concerned, but one of them did come back to me the next day to thank me for the rebuke. Let us continue in faithful service to the One who called us. Let us strive for holiness and delight in the part we have been given by God, to make His holiness shown here on earth. Hallowed be Thy Name!

## ASR Gavin Dickson

Day in, day out, the Lord's Name is used in all sorts of blasphemous ways. I work within the army and I hear His Name bandied about and used as a curse. One thing that worries me more than when those who don't know the Lord take His Name in vain is when those who claim to belong to Him do the same.

I was once sitting in a church meeting where the person leading not only used foul language but openly used the Lord's Name as a curse. This is shocking, but is it uncommon? In some quarters I often hear that there is too little emphasis on God's holiness, on just how wonderful it is that a thrice-holy God saves unholy sinners. Some might be tempted to limit what they say about God's holiness to make it 'easier' for the soldiers to hear; but this does the opposite. It hides the true message we must convey: 'a holy God loves sinners so much He sent Jesus Christ to die on a cross for them.' That is shocking, shockingly wonderful!

## ASR Nick Wilson

Neil, a WO1, has been a Christian for only two months. On my fourth visit to encourage him, he said he was struck by how awesome God is, but shocked by how many people address Him as their 'buddy'. He realized that God's Name should be hallowed and he was challenged to truly revere Him, remembering that, yes, He is loving and merciful, but He is also equally just and holy.

### ASR Ray Hendricks

The sovereignty of God has always been a sticking point when sharing the Word of God with soldiers. While there is nothing here on earth that can be compared to God, He has made many things and systems in His likeness. The United Kingdom with Her Majesty the Queen as sovereign head is one similarity. Not all analogies work, but the intention is to get through to the hearer that God's name is to be 'hallowed', which means He is holy and separated from the sinful world. It is because of this separation that God had to mount His rescue plan for His lost children, the human race, and send Jesus Christ to pay the ransom, or the penalty, for our sins. Soldiers can understand the basic idea that Her Majesty is separated from the rest of the population and that anyone approaching her must be given permission or be invited to meet her and be in her presence. If a soldier had to meet her, he or she would be instructed on how to approach her and all the rules that should not be broken. Jesus is the only One who can instruct us on how to relate to the sovereignty of God's holy Name because Jesus is the only One who knows and has paid the price for us to return to God. And His instruction is simple: to declare the Name of our Father in heaven to be holy, in our words and in our works.

## ASR Meg Atkinson

Sport has always been a great means of getting alongside my troops. Hockey, netball, football, to name but a few: I always enjoyed them and got stuck in. Language on the sports field can be very colourful, and during a cup-final football game one of my team mates was badly tackled. The Lord's Name was mentioned several times in the outburst of protest. 'Don't blame Him, it was number 10 who floored you!' I said cheekily. Later, over refreshments after the game, a discussion developed as to why people do not revere God's Name. 'Meg, we never hear you blaspheme—why not?' 'It all comes down to what kind of relationship we have with God,' I replied. This gave me an opportunity to say why I hold the Name of the Lord to be hallowed, holy. It really challenged them.

# 4. Your kingdom come

Near the end of the Bible, when Jesus returns and gets rid of all the evil in the world, we read this: 'The kingdom of the world has become the kingdom of our Lord and of his Messiah, and he will reign for ever and ever' (Revelation 11:15). One day the kingdom of the Father, ruled over by Jesus, will swallow up all the kingdoms of this world. Then goodness will have completely defeated evil. There will be no more darkness, and life will even swallow up death.

> See, I will create
> > new heavens and a new earth.
> The former things will not be remembered,
> > nor will they come to mind.
> But be glad and rejoice for ever
> > in what I will create,
> for I will create Jerusalem to be a delight
> > and its people a joy.
> I will rejoice over Jerusalem
> > and take delight in my people;
> the sound of weeping and of crying
> > will be heard in it no more (Isaiah 65:17–19).

When the kingdom of God comes in its fullness, *then* there will be no death, no pain, no sorrow and no sadness. When the kingdom of our heavenly Father comes in its fullness on earth, everything that is wrong with the world will be put right: all injustice will end; all selfishness and evil will be driven out for ever and ever.

> With righteousness he will judge the needy,
> > with justice he will give decisions for the poor of
> > the earth.

He will strike the earth with the rod of his mouth;
　　with the breath of his lips he will slay the wicked.
Righteousness will be his belt
　　and faithfulness the sash round his waist.
The wolf will live with the lamb,
　　the leopard will lie down with the goat,
the calf and the lion and the yearling together;
　　and a little child will lead them.
The cow will feed with the bear,
　　their young will lie down together,
　　and the lion will eat straw like the ox.
The infant will play near the cobra's den,
　　and the young child will put its hand into the viper's
　　nest.
They will neither harm nor destroy
　　on all my holy mountain,
for the earth will be filled with the knowledge of
　　the LORD
　　as the waters cover the sea (Isaiah 11:4–9).

When God's kingdom is perfectly present here on earth, *then* there will be nothing wrong with the world ever again. This is why we so urgently pray, every day, 'Your kingdom come'. Every day, we need to be reminded that *this* present world order is not the end of the story. The pain, disappointment, sin and suffering we face right now do not have to be the final word. There is a great *hope* given to everybody who becomes a citizen of the kingdom of God— the certain hope of final victory, of life that never ends, of resurrection beyond death, of the triumph of good over evil.

I saw 'a new heaven and a new earth', for the first
heaven and the first earth had passed away, and there

was no longer any sea. I saw the Holy City, the new Jerusalem, coming down out of heaven from God, prepared as a bride beautifully dressed for her husband. And I heard a loud voice from the throne saying, 'Look! God's dwelling-place is now among the people, and he will dwell with them. They will be his people, and God himself will be with them and be their God. "He will wipe every tear from their eyes. There will be no more death" or mourning or crying or pain, for the old order of things has passed away.'

He who was seated on the throne said, 'I am making everything new!' Then he said, 'Write this down, for these words are trustworthy and true' (Revelation 21:1–5).

Many live this life without any real hope at all. We all meet people who look for hope in their work, in entertainment, in a beautiful home, in sport, in fitness, in family, in retirement or in shopping. In the cold light of day those things are obviously not the answer, but they give us just enough 'hope' to keep us going. If we do not know the Living God, can there be any real hope? The criminal who died next to Jesus needed a better hope than that offered by the kingdoms of this world. He simply looked at Jesus and said, 'Remember me when you come into *your* kingdom' (Luke 23:42, emphasis added). That criminal needed something far more lasting and substantial than anything the kingdoms of *this* world could offer: he needed the hope of God's kingdom, the kingdom of heaven. Jesus told that dying criminal, 'Today you will be with me in paradise' (v. 43). Jesus promised this apparently hopeless man that they would be together within hours in the 'third heaven', where the Father sits in light, life and glory. Although the fullness of the kingdom awaits the final day of resurrection, on that very day, after all the agony of his death, the thief entered into the glorious experience of God's kingdom that is already enjoyed by all those who wait in heaven.

The Living God made us for so much more than this passing life, for so much more than running round the hamster wheel of the kingdoms of this world. Yes, the kingdoms of this world want us to be satisfied with their *little* treats and their *little* hopes, but the kingdom of God calls us to be citizens of a much greater kingdom. The kingdom of God is a kingdom that takes anybody and everybody, especially those who are *least* in the kingdoms of this world. The kingdom of God gives real hope and dignity, life and purpose, no matter who we are, how weak or foolish we are, or how messed up we are. In the church, we are citizens of the kingdom of God. In church, we live something of that life of God's kingdom *right now*, even before the end of the world. The very first words that Jesus preached were about the kingdom of God. Matthew 4:17 describes how Jesus began to tell the world His big news:

> From that time on Jesus began to preach, 'Repent, for the kingdom of heaven has come near.'

His kingdom is the heavenly kingdom. *Jesus* is the King of God's kingdom. One of the things that sometimes puzzles Bible students is that Jesus speaks about the kingdom of God all the way through His teaching, but the apostles hardly ever mention the kingdom of God directly. At times, unstable Bible scholars have developed the most bizarre theories to deal with this fact. The truth is that it is not only the apostles but all of God's people, before and after Jesus, who display this same approach. None of us speaks of the kingdom of God as much as Jesus did. The fact is this: *Jesus* talked about the kingdom all the time, but *we* talk about the King all the time. When we look at the kingdom of God our attention is always grabbed by the King, by the One who makes it all possible. As the King of the kingdom He speaks about His kingdom all the time; but as citizens of this kingdom we speak about the King all the time.

In one sense, when we ask for the Father's kingdom to come, we are asking for the King to come. We are yearning for King Jesus to return to the world to put everything right. The kingdom of God is all about the reign of the King. That is the key to understanding the kingdom of heaven. The kingdom of heaven is the heavens and the earth under the rule of the Living God through Jesus, in the power of the Spirit. The Bible describes how all the animals look to Him for their food; how He clothes even the plants and the flowers with beauty; how He names and organizes all the stars across the universe; how the oceans obey His rules; how the lightning goes just where He tells it to go. In other words, the whole of the heavens and the earth looks to the throne in heaven where the Father sits with His Son and His Spirit, giving life and purpose to everything, even in this age of turmoil and darkness. The rule of heaven covers all of history and all of creation, stretching on into an infinite future.

Life in church is life in the kingdom. Even right now we taste the life of the kingdom as we live together as church. While we wait for the coming of the King, we already experience His kingdom when we trust ourselves to Him each day, when we say 'no' to the deceitful desires of this passing age and 'yes' to practical love, justice and righteousness. Local church is supposed to be heaven on earth, a real experience of the kingdom of heaven right in the middle of this passing darkness. Our churches can be beacons of light offering genuine hope and help in a world where people have no hope and feel so helpless. If we want to know the kingdom of God in our own hearts and lives, the first step is to commit ourselves to the expression of that kingdom which is our local church. There the reign of God becomes visible and tangible right now as we await the coming of the King. There, in our churches, the Spirit is at work to change lives and to teach us to obey all that Christ the King commanded. If we claim to be citizens of the kingdom of heaven, we should live lives worthy of that status, as Paul told the church at Philippi:

> Above all, you must live as citizens of heaven, conducting yourselves in a manner worthy of the Good News about Christ. Then, whether I come and see you again or only hear about you, I will know that you are standing together with one spirit and one purpose, fighting together for the faith, which is the Good News (Philippians 1:27, NLT).

The mission of the local church is to show and grow the kingdom of God. The weekly prayer meeting is nothing less than an invasion of the kingdom of heaven into the kingdoms of this world! The kingdom of God advances when we refuse to obey the orders of the principalities and powers of this passing age and instead show that we trust the orders and authority of the throne of heaven where King Jesus sits alongside the glorious Father. Sometimes individual Christians try to go on 'solo missions' to advance God's kingdom, but that is rarely effective and may in fact be quite destructive. The power of God's kingdom is His church, the great army of heaven on earth. When we work together, under the authority structures of church that He has appointed, then all our gifts can come together, through the power and gifts of the Spirit. Then our battle against the powers of this age may bring about an extraordinary harvest as our churches turn the world upside down!

Yet the kingdom of heaven is opposed by other kingdoms, by human kingdoms of this world, and even by devilish rulers of spiritual kingdoms. Within the heavens and the earth there are pockets of rebellion, forces of darkness, chaos and evil, where the devil has enslaved humanity in his futile war against the Living God. On New Year's Day 2011 there was a riot at Ford Open Prison in West Sussex. There was a strong suspicion that alcohol had been smuggled into the prison for the New Year and so the authorities had decided to do breathalyser tests on the prisoners. Forty prisoners began a riot, smashing windows and setting off alarms. This spread to other buildings which were set on fire. In the end, eight blocks in the prison were burnt to the ground, including the gym and snooker facilities. The prison staff had to leave the site, and order was restored only when specialist officers in riot gear with police support were brought in. Think of that island of lawlessness and chaos in West Sussex during that riot. It was shaking its fist at the peace and order of the surrounding world. That is how the rebellion of this world and its kingdoms looks from the perspective of heaven. The devil is the ringleader of the riot but all men and women are enthusiastic followers. We join in the riot, each generation carrying on with the selfishness, destruction and darkness. In each generation we act as if there is no kingdom of heaven, no purpose, no law, no meaning to our lives. We act as if we can do what we want, and we even become angry if anybody tells us what to do.

Yet a day is coming when peace and order will be restored; when the world will be cleaned up; when the destruction will be repaired; when this whole rebellion will be thrown out and shut out for ever and ever. The forces of justice and goodness are coming: a day has been set. The King is coming, riding on a white horse, surrounded by all the armies of heaven; and in a moment all the forces of evil will be defeated.

> I saw heaven standing open and there before me was
> a white horse, whose rider is called Faithful and True.
> With justice he judges and wages war. His eyes are like
> blazing fire, and on his head are many crowns. He has a
> name written on him that no one knows but he himself.
> He is dressed in a robe dipped in blood, and his name is
> the Word of God. The armies of heaven were following
> him, riding on white horses and dressed in fine linen,
> white and clean. Coming out of his mouth is a sharp
> sword with which to strike down the nations. 'He will
> rule them with an iron sceptre.' He treads the winepress
> of the fury of the wrath of God Almighty. On his robe
> and on his thigh he has this name written: KING OF
> KINGS AND LORD OF LORDS (Revelation 19:11–16).

How wonderful it is to look forward to the final and complete triumph of good over evil! How much easier we can sleep knowing that, no matter how much evil and darkness rage against light and life, the end is already written, the victory is certain! Jesus will defeat all the forces of evil with the mere breath of His mouth. When the Divine Warrior comes out to wage war for His kingdom, the war will be won in a single moment. With this in mind we need to surrender ourselves completely to Him and find peace in Him.

> Suppose a king is about to go to war against another king. Won't he first sit down and consider whether he is able with ten thousand men to oppose the one coming against him with twenty thousand? If he is not able, he will send a delegation while the other is still a long way off and will ask for terms of peace (Luke 14: 31–32).

When Jesus speaks of His kingdom He speaks much about this big picture of history and the kingdoms of this world. His parables are filled with reminders of the way history will end when His kingdom conquers the world. Jesus speaks to us as if we are in a prison siege; as if we are rioting prisoners; as if the riot police of heaven are already gathering at the gates; as if our only hope is to surrender and join the kingdom of heaven before that army arrives. If we will not—if we continue with the prison riot, if we think anything else is worth more than the kingdom— there can be only one outcome: *we will have no place to go in death and no safe place to run to on that final day. That* day is the day we long for, because *then* everything will be made right; the lights will be switched on and all our tears will be wiped away by the Lord God Himself.

Each day we pray for the coming of the kingdom. The whole Bible ends with this simple prayer: 'Come, Lord Jesus'. Every day we need to be reminded that this world is not the end of the story: the pain and suffering we face right now do not have to be the final word. Just as our Father is in heaven, so there is a kingdom of goodness and truth, purity and dignity, beyond all the sordid and failing kingdoms of this world.

# *Reflections*

## ASR William Wade

As I speak with soldiers about the gospel, an attempt is often made to sideline the conversation with red herrings such as 'Did Adam have a belly button?', 'What about the dinosaurs?' or even 'Do you think there are aliens?' Soldiers are happy to speak about the ethereal and the abstract without committing to the historical reality of Jesus Christ. However, in evangelism, there needs to be a personal engagement: a sense of contact with the person you are speaking with.

One way I like to make that contact is to pray with a soldier, right there and then. Instead of telling a soldier that I will pray in a church or at a later date, if there is an issue that needs to be prayed for (such as an imminent deployment to a dangerous location, a relationship difficulty, a court case, etc.), then I ask that soldier if I can pray for that situation right there and then. I have asked hundreds of soldiers, and, over almost fourteen years now, not one has ever said 'no'.

The reason I pray there and then is twofold: first, the soldier will know that a Christian cared enough to pray; and, second, more often than not there is a tangible sense of the presence of God, no matter what the context—be it in a gym, on the exercise area, or in a trench. This type of on-the-spot prayer allows the kingdom of God to come into the otherwise 'normal' routine of military life. This kind of prayer brings the soldier face to face with the reality of the presence of God, and I have had many a soldier describe a sense of peace as a prayer is made for him or her. It is also a great opportunity to give further witness of the peace which a life in Jesus can bring. Thank God that, no matter where it might be and in whatever context, the kingdom of God can still come, even in the most surprising of circumstances!

## ASR Roddy MacLeod

As a Scripture Reader I spend all my time asking people to consider the coming kingdom of the Lord Jesus Christ. The vast majority have no idea at all that this kingdom is revealed in the most wonderful and glorious way in the words of the Holy Bible. I find that many soldiers, when you start to scratch the surface, are interested to know about the kingdom, and they listen with interest. I can speak confidently to individuals, old and young, small and large groups, and congregations of soldiers, knowing that the truth, the words of God, will not return to Him void.

On one occasion, I was hugely encouraged to see God's work and seeds grow. A lady, who was a Commonwealth soldier and a Christian, told me of another soldier she had met. In her phase-two training she had come across a young man who asked her to tell him about the Bible. For a while she discussed God with this soldier, and at the end of the conversation she asked him why he wanted to know these things.

He told her that when he came to Pirbright he was an atheist, but there he had met 'Roddy', who shared the gospel with him—and now he believes it! I don't know anything about this man, not even his name, but I pray for him. I'm certain there are many other stories like ours out there. The Lord works in wondrous ways to further His kingdom.

## ASR Gavin Dickson

In our weekly soldiers' Bible study we were once looking at how to be a man of God, going through a book called *The Measure of a Man*, which takes Paul's teaching to Timothy and Titus and applies it to all men. We were discussing anger and how to act with a godly response to anger. ASR Lee McDade reminded us of eternity, saying that Christians often suffer from eternity amnesia, forgetting that this earth is but fleeting and that there is an eternity with Jesus to look forward to. This refocused our minds and brought our group to worship the Lord in heartfelt prayer with a fresh kingdom perspective.

## ASR David Murray

When talking to soldiers I use the word 'heaven', which most of them understand. However, whenever the word 'kingdom' is used, nobody has heard it in this context. It has to be explained to them that we must get into this kingdom of God; that it's not a place (yet), but those who come to faith in Christ will be accepted into God's kingdom here on earth. A kingdom for believers, a spiritual kingdom.

## ASR & Area Rep Paul Somerville

I entered a barracks room and met a young Royal Navy sailor who was on detachment to the unit accompanying an RN helicopter as ground crew. He was sitting before a computer screen playing a game and he invited me to join him. He explained that the aim of the game was to create your own world, your own perfect kingdom, and the strategy was to put in place laws, balancing spending, and doing all the things necessary to create the perfect world to live in.

He took me on a tour around his fictional perfect kingdom, pointing out several points of interest in his world. He showed me the football stadiums, the theatres, the cinemas—all for entertainment. He pointed out the schools for education and the huge farms that provided more than enough food for the people of his world. I complimented him on his vision and ideas, and I then pointed to other items on the screen and asked what they were. 'Oh, that's the police station, the hospital and the cemetery,' he said.

I said to the young sailor that his 'perfect' kingdom wasn't that perfect if he had to factor in these places to accommodate crime, illness and death. I pointed out that this will always be the story of humanity:

that our past is full of sin, our present is steeped in sorrow, and all that awaits us in the future is death. But this gave me the opportunity to share that there is an answer to our problem, and that answer is found in the Lord Jesus Christ—He who came to declare 'My kingdom is at hand'.

### ASR Meg Atkinson

I was sitting at a table in a T bar with a number of guys and one girl. The young airwoman said she wanted to believe, having been an altar server as a little girl, but she couldn't because of all the sadness in the world. That statement got the whole table of guys chipping in. One airman said he would rather go to hell, believing it to be better than the here and now. I read from Luke 16:19–31, then contrasted that with the picture in Revelation 21, and asked if a place of separation and torment was better than a place of no pain, no tears and no grief. It was good to leave several pieces of literature for them to read in their own time, and to encourage them to contemplate a kingdom to come, in God's timing.

# 5. Your will be done on earth as it is in heaven

None of us likes to be told what to do. In fact, one of the most common attitudes of our age is 'nobody tells me what to do'. Yet in the Lord's Prayer we pray every day that we will do what we are told: that we will do what *the Father* wills, rather than what *we* will. In many ways this is the hardest part to pray. We like life to be the way *we* want, the way *we* choose, but every day we pray, 'Actually, I want to do it *Your* way.' The deep issue here is this: *you are your own worst enemy*. The natural me, the flesh-and-blood me, the Paul Blackham who was born by human will and desire, is my worst enemy! That me is selfish, godless and full of deceitful desires. My flesh wants to please itself, and whenever I am hungry, angry, lonely or tired those base desires and instincts often get behind the steering wheel of my life.

Many people get drunk on Friday and Saturday nights *deliberately* so that they can let their flesh go and give free reign to those base desires without feeling responsible for them. They want to do *their own* will, and the will of the most holy Father in heaven is very far from their thoughts. Jesus said that if we try to cling on to our natural life we will lose whatever life we have and we will die. *If our own will is in the driving seat we will not only crash many times as we go through life, but we will actually end up driving off the cliff into the eternity of hell*. We need to die and rise again before that happens; we need to be born again, to begin our life again in a very different way with a different kind of life in us. We all need the life of somebody else, somebody who is the very opposite of our natural selfish life. That is what Jesus is all about. That is why *His* dying and rising again are the centre of church life. *He* has made it possible for us to die to ourselves and receive His new kind of human life that He brought back from the dead.

He bore the divine punishment for all the wrong we have ever done so that all that wrong could be done away with once and for all. He confronted our mess in His death so it could be taken away. He made it possible for our sin to be forgiven so that we need no longer be separated from the life of God. He took our old life and exchanged it for His perfect ever-new life by the wonderful wisdom of the Father in His birth, life, death, resurrection and ascension. Hear how Paul explains all this in Colossians 2:11–15:

> Your whole self ruled by the flesh was put off when you were circumcised by Christ, having been buried with him in baptism, in which you were also raised with him through your faith in the working of God, who raised him from the dead.

> When you were dead in your sins and in the uncircumcision of your flesh, God made you alive with Christ. He forgave us all our sins, having cancelled the charge of our legal indebtedness, which stood against us and condemned us; he has taken it away, nailing it to the cross. And having disarmed the powers and authorities, he made a public spectacle of them, triumphing over them by the cross.

That is the big stuff that is included in that daily prayer, 'Your will be done on earth as it is in heaven.'

Let's tackle a deep question. The Bible tells us that Jesus defeated the devil at the cross. In fact, the Bible says that

Jesus made a mockery of the devil and all the demons when He died on the cross. So *how* did Jesus defeat the devil by dying on the cross? *Why* does dying such a terrible death make a mockery of the devil and the demons? Let's leave that question stewing in our brains for a while—but don't forget it! Let's instead turn to another question, a question that might seem easier to answer. In the Lord's Prayer we pray, 'Heavenly Father, may Your will be done on earth *as it is in heaven.' How is the will of the Father done in heaven?* In heaven, *how* do the angels and the triumphant people of God respond to the will of the Father? Let's read from Revelation 4 to find out:

> In the centre, round the throne, were four living creatures, and they were covered with eyes, in front and behind. The first living creature was like a lion, the second was like an ox, the third had a face like a man, the fourth was like a flying eagle. Each of the four living creatures had six wings and was covered with eyes all round, even under its wings. Day and night they never stop saying:
>
> '"Holy, holy, holy
> is the Lord God Almighty",
> who was, and is, and is to come.'
>
> Whenever the living creatures give glory, honour and thanks to him who sits on the throne and who lives for ever and ever, the twenty-four elders fall down before him who sits on the throne and worship him who lives for ever and ever. They lay their crowns before the throne and say:
>
> 'You are worthy, our Lord and God,
>     to receive glory and honour and power,

for you created all things,
    and *by your will they were created*
    *and have their being* (Revelation 4:6–11, emphasis added).

Notice that when the worship of heaven builds up to a climax it is the *will* of the Father that everyone in heaven appreciates. The will of the Father makes everything possible, in heaven and on earth. The will of the Father is the reason why everything was created in the beginning, and it is also the reason why everything still exists. The will of the Father holds everything together, through Jesus, by the power of the Spirit.

> The twenty-four elders fall down before him who sits on the throne and worship him who lives for ever and ever. They lay their crowns before the throne and say:
>
> 'You are worthy, our Lord and God,
>     to receive glory and honour and power,
> for you created all things,
>     and *by your will* they were created
>     and have their being.

Together with all the angelic creatures, the representatives of all the humans in heaven acknowledge the *will* of the Father as the reason why He should be worshipped and glorified. Why? Why be so excited and enthusiastic about the will of the Father? Because they trust Him utterly. As we read through the book of Revelation we see that history is not straightforward! Present throughout that book—throughout the whole of history—there is the devil. He is portrayed as a terrible dragon, and under his control are beasts that represent false religion and human political power. We see how countless Christians are killed for following Jesus. We see how injustice, disease, war and death are constantly riding across the world throughout history. The four horsemen are always riding, sent from heaven to bring judgement on the world. It might feel as if history is out of control, but in fact everything is ruled by the will of the Father. As we read Revelation we see that everything is always under the will of the Father. Always at the centre is the *Father* with the Lord Jesus; and no matter what angle we choose to consider history from, *the Lamb always wins*: Jesus is always the winner. All those who trust the Father find themselves safe in His keeping, and even if they die, they are caught up to be with Him in that glorious paradise of the third heaven. *In heaven there is absolute trust in the will of the Father.* No matter how bad things might look from time to time, there is total trust that His will is best; that after suffering there will be glory; that after this passing age, after the kingdoms of this world, is the *coming kingdom* of God.

In heaven, the Father's will is loved and trusted, and all the angels and all the humans in heaven always obey His will with joy and trust. So we pray that His will would be done on earth just as it is in heaven. We pray that we would love, trust and obey the will of the Father on earth just as all the hundreds of millions do in heaven. Jesus always had that attitude to His Father. One of the most powerful verses in the whole Bible is John 4:34, where Jesus said, 'My food … is to do the will of him who sent me and to finish his work.' *Jesus loved to be told what to do.* He loved to do His Father's will and to finish *His* work. Jesus did not ever like to please Himself or do His own thing.

I don't think anything else shows how different Jesus is from natural human beings. *I want to please myself, but Jesus loved to be told what to do.* We might have had all kinds of reasons for not trusting our earthly father, but when we know the heavenly Father through Jesus, we know that we can always trust His will. Look at how Jesus faced the ultimate test of that trust in the Garden of Gethsemane just before He went to die by crucifixion. His body wanted to run away and protect itself. Emotionally, he was terrified of all the pain and humiliation that was to come. More than these things, He knew He was going to face the anger of heaven. Jesus was about to become sin. He was about to become everything that His Father hates, everything that is offensive to heaven, everything that He Himself hated. Jesus was going to take responsibility for the mess you and I have made of our lives, and therefore He was going to get what *we* deserve. *This* was what His Father had sent Him to do so that we might escape from our selfish mess and receive the kind of life Jesus had always enjoyed with His Father. So Jesus faced the moment of decision. He could call ten thousand angels to save Him and be carried back to the eternal glory of heaven, or He could keep obeying His Father's will to the very end, *trusting* His Father's will, no matter how far that went. Philippians 2:8–9 puts this clearly: 'He humbled himself by becoming obedient to death—even death on a cross! Therefore God exalted him to the highest place and gave him the name that is above every name.' By being obedient to the Father's will, trusting Him no matter what—even to such an extreme—Jesus established a new kind of life based on trust in the Father, where suffering and sacrifice are true glory.

*This* was the collision with the devil at the most basic level. Satan constantly wants us to please ourselves. He always wants us to do what *we* want to do, to refuse to do the will of anybody else. *Satan wants us to serve* his *will by following our own will.* When Jesus insisted that He had to go to the cross to suffer and die, Peter was angry and upset. *No!* The meaning of life could not be about suffering! We want to run away from suffering. We want to get as many years of health and wealth as we possibly can, and the idea of deliberately running into suffering seems utterly wrong. Peter was sure that Jesus should *not* go to the cross. Instead, He should become the popular leader of the world, and the apostles should be the powerful leaders in Christ's new kingdom. When Peter told Jesus not to go to the cross, what did Jesus say? 'Get behind me, *Satan!*' (Matthew 16:23). When Peter was trying to put self-protection above self-sacrifice, Jesus immediately recognized whose voice, whose mind, was at work. Peter was devoured by the devil when he wanted to avoid the obedience and sacrifice that is the way of Jesus. When it came to the time of Jesus' torture and death, Peter could not face it. He was still controlled by the old flesh—by the desire to look after himself and find a comfortable life. So Peter denied any relationship to Jesus at all—three times! Peter was not ready to say, '*Your* will, not mine.'

At the end of John's Gospel, after Jesus had died and came back to life, Jesus told Peter that one day he too would die by crucifixion. Peter spent his life knowing that the will of the Father for him was to face the very kind of suffering and death he had been so desperate to escape. So what kind of life did Peter lead? We might think he would have led a life of morbid obsessions, worrying about the terrible death that lay in his future. But no! Peter describes this new life of Jesus, the life of obedience to the Father's will, as 'inexpressible and glorious joy' (1 Peter 1:8). Incredible! The more Peter learned to embrace the will of the Father, the more Peter knew joy and glory.

Each day we pray that the Father's will might be done on earth as in heaven. In this deep prayer, we are kneeling with the Lord Jesus in the Garden of Gethsemane—'Your will be done, not my will.' We could never win that battle or pray that prayer if Jesus had not first won that battle for us. We don't become right with God by learning to trust and obey; *Jesus* makes us right with God, no matter how badly we mess up in life. Yet, when we follow Jesus, He teaches us the revolution of finding our food and drink in obeying the Father's will.

So let's go back to that deep question we asked at the beginning: How did Jesus make a mockery of the devil at the cross? The devil has bet everything on selfishness. The devil passionately believes in pleasing yourself, doing what you want, refusing to do what God wills. The world is enslaved to the devil's lie and our natural instinct is always to look after ourselves and do what we want. The devil tells us that we must grasp all the experiences and possessions we can in *this* life because, he says, God wants to keep good things from us. The Father sent Jesus to set us free from that lie, to show that it is the devil who has brought the suffering and death into the world; that in fact the Living God only wants to take us into that joy and life of His presence and into a renewed world that lasts for ever. So Jesus came to live our life right here in this world where the flesh and the devil have such power. Jesus refused to do His own will at any time. He held firm to only ever following the Father's will—*even* at the very hardest point; even when following the Father's will would cut Him off from the Father on the cross. Jesus refused to follow His own will—and by doing that He opened the way for all of humanity to enter into life, for free and for ever. Jesus received the name that is above every name because He refused to put Himself first; He refused to assert His own will; but rather He looked always to the Father's will and to the power of the Spirit. On the cross Jesus mocked the selfishness of the devil. He was openly showing that the devil's way was a failure, that the Father's will leads to true glory, joy and goodness. The devil must have been shocked that the immortal Son was determined to do the will of the Father, even if it meant a cursed death on the cross. Yet the fact that Jesus, the Author of Life, would do *that* exposed the lie of the devil once and for all. The resurrection and ascension of Jesus publicly showed the victory over the devil's selfishness that Jesus won at the cross.

Each day we pray that we would put the old flesh to death and that we would follow Jesus—that we would do the Father's will just as it is done in heaven. Each day we ask that we would be set free from the lie of the devil and trust our heavenly Father. True freedom and dignity come when we are set free from ourselves. The Father's will is guided by infinite wisdom and love. Our own will is clouded by selfishness and short-sightedness, even at the very best of times. It is when we trust the Father that we discover the freedom to live fruitful and fulfilled lives. Every day we need to crucify our flesh and follow the way of Jesus. 'Father, may Your will be done on earth in my life, just as it is in heaven.'

# Reflections

## ASR & Area Rep Paul Somerville

I was standing chatting to two AAC lads when another soldier appeared; they introduced me as a Christian to him. I wasn't sure why they did so, but I later found out that this soldier was pretty antagonistic towards every religious belief, especially Christianity. This soldier, called Paul, though polite in his manner, began to tell me why the Bible was an unreliable source for mankind and how Jesus was a myth. He shared with me his theories, quoting prominent authors like Dawkins.

While Paul was sharing this with me I was rummaging around in my mind formulating arguments with which to counter his. I was listening with one ear and yet getting ready to counter with a verbal left hook and maybe an uppercut or two. Then a thought dropped into my mind: 'So you win the argument … then what?'

I was still staring at Paul, giving the outward impression that I was listening, but my attention had been caught by that thought. I don't usually hear voices in my head, but that evening, standing in front of this soldier, I heard the words 'Tell him about me'. When Paul paused for breath, I asked, 'Can I tell you about Jesus?' He said that Jesus was a myth and that the Bible could be disproved. Oh, how I had my uppercut ready! But instead I continued by saying,

'Well, let me share with you about Him, just as you have shared your view with me.'

Paul listened as I told him about my Saviour: who He is, why He came, where He is now. I had never had a conversation with a soldier in such a manner before; around us was noise and distraction, but between us was a vacuum, and all that could be heard was my voice carrying to him the greatest story ever told: the story of Jesus. Paul looked at me when I paused for breath and his next words floored me: he unleashed his uppercut ... but in a nice way! He asked me if I would come with him right then, back to his ops rooms to meet his colleagues, and tell them what I had just told him, because he had never heard it put like that before. So I accompanied him back to the helicopter ops rooms and spoke to a gathered audience about my Saviour, leaving them some literature. It was a profitable evening and my intentions that evening, no matter how plausible, were overruled by His will.

## ASR & Area Rep Steve Penny

One afternoon I was speaking about the work of SASRA at a local church when an elderly lady came up to me to say how much she had been inspired by the work of SASRA over the years. She explained that she also prayed for the outreach work among young people on the streets of her town at night. As an elderly lady, she normally gathered with others in the church to pray while the outreach team went out into the town centre at night. One evening she felt the Lord's call to go out to join the outreach team. It was not what she wanted to do as it was a cold, dark night and she wasn't confident going out, but she felt that this was the Lord's will. Upon venturing out, with someone helping her, the first person she spoke to was a young soldier who was about to be deployed to Afghanistan. As she talked to him, he said that he was fearful of what might happen to him on deployment, especially as he didn't know where he would go when he died. This lady was able to pray with him and help him to understand the assurance of salvation that is available to us when we believe. If she hadn't obeyed the will of God, this would not have happened.

## ASR Paul Curd

When the reality of becoming an Army Scripture Reader first began to dawn in my mind it seemed to me a far-fetched idea, but one that wouldn't let me go. Here I was, forty-five years old, having achieved not that much (to my way of thinking) and feeling as if I had somehow 'missed the boat'. At this point my only experience of a Scripture Reader was with Ivor Sherwood while at Gütersloh in Germany during my last year in the army in 1994. At that point I didn't really understand what a Scripture Reader was for, but I was very impressed: Ivor and May were an amazing couple and a real support during a tough year. Ivor ran a Sunday church meeting and always seemed to know the right 'spiritual' thing to say. Could I ever live up to that? I mean, me? an evangelist?! I hadn't a clue how to speak to people about Christ! Anyway, I decided to let God be God, as only He knows what is right and best for us. I decided to trust Him by placing the whole application process in His hands. This is the safest place to be: within His will and within His purposes. With some encouragement from my church I went ahead and applied. I 'pushed at the door'. When that hurdle was passed, I pushed at the next ... and the next! Each time I prayed, 'Lord, if this is not Your will, I don't want it. But if it is, then You will need to help me, as I don't feel equipped for this role.'

As it turned out, God knew what He was doing! After a period of mentoring, once I was left to get on with the job at Pirbright, I found that with every conversation and in each circumstance, God was with me. I truly felt His leading and equipping. What is more, whenever I had the privilege of ministering the gospel into someone's life, it seemed to make sense to that person. Glory to God! I also discovered, with hindsight, that God had been preparing me all along. It seems to me that the most important thing any of us believers can do is to seek His sovereign will. We must never presume to think that we know best, or that we 'have what it takes': we must 'let go, and let God'.

## ASR Meg Atkinson

Having enjoyed a good banter in the T bar with a group of airmen and shared Easter Creme Eggs with them all, I took my leave, leaving behind some Easter booklets in case anyone should choose to read them. As I walked across the hangar, Justin shouted to get my attention. 'I love your booklets! I sneak them in my pocket when nobody's looking and read them in my room.' I asked if they had any effect on him, and he said they caused him to go and see a 'Jesus film' at the cinema. I asked if the film pointed out the importance of the resurrection: it didn't, it just made mention of it. After much discussion, we prayed together and Justin received Christ as his Saviour.

On my next visit to the hangar I asked Justin if his commitment had made any difference to him: 'Yes, Jesus is the pillion passenger on my motorbike, so I ride my bike in a more thoughtful way, considering how Jesus would think and act towards others.' Justin was earnestly seeking God's will, even in the small things!

## ASR Roddy MacLeod

I was speaking to a young Christian soldier who told me he had met a girl who wasn't a Christian. He was looking to God for guidance as to what he should do: to go out with this girl or not. I spoke to him from 2 Corinthians about not being 'unequally yoked' with unbelievers, and that righteousness and light cannot be partners with lawlessness and darkness. After what seemed a long time spent discussing these matters he said he would need to seek God's guidance. Unfortunately, what I showed the soldier from the Bible didn't suit him. In essence, he wanted his own will to be done, not the Lord's. Sometimes it is with a heavy heart that we do our work for the Lord.

## ASR Gavin Dickson

Some opportunities come and need to be grabbed with both hands, but there are times when opportunities pass by for reasons we don't always understand. I had two 'missed' or 'untaken' opportunities recently.

One was when I was invited to take part in a four-mile run with the Light Dragoons and to talk about Christ for a few minutes beforehand. The other was when, after taking part in the RDG's Carol Service, I was invited to their Christmas meal. Both of these would have been great opportunities to get my face known in each battalion, but the Lord had me doing other things. Then there are the opportunities that are taken, such as playing rugby for the officer's mess of the Royal Lancers, and taking part in the 2Yorks Fijian Celebration day. Both these opportunities led to me being able to share the gospel and strengthened my ability to come alongside soldiers as well as build respect for sharing the good news at later dates. With both missed and taken opportunities my prayer must be that the Lord's will be done, otherwise I am resting in my own strength and not the Lord's.

### ASR David Murray

When speaking to a group of soldiers I took them to 2 Timothy 2:1–7 where the Word tells us that the Lord Jesus Christ is our 'commanding officer', that we should therefore obey Him (do His will), and that He only wants the best for His soldiers. After all, every soldier must obey his or her commanding officer or there will be a penalty to pay. The soldiers understand military language so this helped them better understand the authority of God and how we need to know and carry out His will.

# 6. Give us this day our daily bread

What do we need each day? Up until this point the Lord's prayer has been looking *upwards*—towards our Father in heaven, towards the coming of the kingdom of heaven, towards the will of God that is properly loved and trusted in heaven. Now we pray that we might get bread for today. It seems like a very definite fall down to earth—to the very earthly and physical requirement for bread. Bread is sometimes called the 'staff of life', a phrase taken from Ezekiel 4:16 and 5:16 in the King James Version of the Bible. Bread is the solid, basic core of food that keeps life going. For most people in the world cereal grains—wheat, rice and so on—are the basic foundation for day-to-day life. So in this part of the Lord's Prayer we get down to the core need of day-to-day life. If we are going to do the will of the Father on earth just as it is done in heaven, we need to have the core thing that will sustain our life. It *sounds* as if we are simply asking for a loaf of bread each day, but is that what we really need most of all? If we are asking for the basic necessities of life, what *do* we need most every day? Let's stop to think about that carefully. What do we *need* each day? When we are caught up in the rat race of materialism and entertainment, it is very hard to see what we really *need*.

On many Saturdays I genuinely believe that one of my key needs is for Everton to get three points—but in my more lucid moments I know how ridiculous such an idea is. I don't *need* anything like that! But what do I really need? Government agencies have different ways of deciding what are the core needs for life. In a disaster zone or in war or famine, the four basic needs are food, water, clothing and shelter. We can all see that clearly. When *everything* has been taken from us, the basics of food, water, clothing and shelter are all we need. However, in more settled situations the needs are expanded to sanitation, education and healthcare. Without basic hygiene, life will rapidly deteriorate; and without healthcare, all kinds of illnesses can develop and become life-threatening. What about education? A primary education is essential because it enables us to read, write and communicate. These really are basic necessities of life, and precisely because the Living God has preserved His revelation in written form, the Bible usually brings education to a society. With education come all kinds of possibilities for life improvement and development.

However, Jesus taught us not to worry about these things. The temptation is to be taken up with these basic necessities of life, but Jesus very carefully and deliberately taught us that we are not to concern ourselves with any of these things.

Listen carefully as you slowly read this radical, wonderful teaching of the Lord Jesus Christ:

> I tell you, do not worry about your life, what you will eat or drink; or about your body, what you will wear. Is not life more than food, and the body more than clothes? Look at the birds of the air; they do not sow or reap or store away in barns, and yet your heavenly Father feeds them. Are you not much more valuable than they? Can any one of you by worrying add a single hour to your life?
>
> And why do you worry about clothes? See how the flowers of the field grow. They do not labour or spin.

Yet I tell you that not even Solomon in all his splendour was dressed like one of these. If that is how God clothes the grass of the field, which is here today and tomorrow is thrown into the fire, will he not much more clothe you—you of little faith? So do not worry, saying, 'What shall we eat?' or 'What shall we drink?' or 'What shall we wear?' For the pagans run after all these things, and your heavenly Father knows that you need them. But seek first his kingdom and his righteousness, and all these things will be given to you as well. Therefore do not worry about tomorrow, for tomorrow will worry about itself. Each day has enough trouble of its own (Matthew 6:25–34).

The point is this: if we are following the Lord Jesus Christ and His kingdom, we do not need to worry about the basic needs of life: food, water and clothing. He specifically states that all these basic needs are fully known to our heavenly Father. If we trust Him each day, we do not need to worry about them at all. Notice that the prayer is 'Give *us* this day our daily bread'. In other words, we are praying not just for our own daily needs, but also for the rest of God's people. We should be concerned for the basic needs of one another, and the answer to our prayer may often mean us sharing what we have with one another. Remember that in Matthew 25 Jesus said that on the final day of judgement the world will be divided up into sheep and goats. The sheep are His people who have clothed the naked, fed the hungry and visited the sick. Our life together as God's people is a life of caring for one another. We are asking our heavenly Father to provide daily bread for all of us *together*. So, yes, each day we pray to our heavenly Father, trusting Him to provide the basic needs of life. However, many Christians starve or die from exposure to the cold. The Bible says that Christians will not usually experience such things, but we do see it happening even in the Bible itself. Around the world today there are Christians facing such challenges. That might make us think a little more deeply about this matter of *daily bread*. Listen again to the words of Jesus in Matthew 6:

> Seek first his kingdom and his righteousness, and all these things will be given to you as well. Therefore do not worry about tomorrow, for tomorrow will worry about itself. Each day has enough trouble of its own.

There is a higher priority than food and drink. There is something that must mean more to us than even the basic needs of food, water and clothing. Jesus and His kingdom is the highest priority of all. We are to seek Him—His kingdom and His righteousness—and leave all the basic needs of the body to our Father's care. When we fast we are reminded of those words of Jesus when He was tempted by the devil: 'Man shall not live on bread alone, but on every word that comes from the mouth of God' (Matthew 4:4). These words come originally from Deuteronomy 8:1–3:

> Be careful to follow every command I am giving you today, so that you may live and increase and may enter and possess the land that the LORD promised on oath to your ancestors. Remember how the LORD your God led you all the way in the wilderness these forty years, to humble and test you in order to know what was in your heart, whether or not you would keep his commands. He humbled you, causing you to hunger and then feeding you with manna, which neither you nor your

ancestors had known, to teach you that man does not
live on bread alone but on every word that comes from
the mouth of the LORD.

The Lord God led His people through a time of hunger
and thirst to see what really mattered to them. He wanted
to know what their true priorities were. Jesus knew that
physical food was not as important as fellowship with
the Living God. He would never sacrifice His close link
with His Father for mere physical food. It would be better
to starve to death rather than lose the Living God. This
takes us back into the deep roots of this phrase 'Give us
today our daily bread'. First, it reminds us that we need
only enough for *today*. Second, it speaks about a *daily*
provision of *bread*. If we have read the first books of the
Bible we might remember how, when God had just rescued
his people from slavery in Egypt, He led them across the
Red Sea into the desert wilderness where there was no
food. They became hungry and even started to grumble.
The Lord said that He had brought them to the desert and
made them hungry to see what was really in their hearts.
Did they love Him? Did they trust Him? Did they really
think He was going to do them harm by bringing them
out to the desert? Did they want to be with Him more than
they wanted all the luxury food of Egypt? These are deep
questions, and they are the same kinds of questions we face
every single day.

Whatever we are facing each day, whatever trials,
temptations or suffering, we face the same question: Do
I trust Jesus to lead me through this day? Do I trust Him
to give me all I need to overcome these temptations, these
challenges? As a church family, do we trust Him to give

us what we need each and every day? In Exodus 16, when God's people were grumbling and hungry in the wilderness, the Lord provided *daily bread* for them. Listen to the story of how it happened—and the warning that came with it:

> … in the morning there was a layer of dew around the camp. When the dew was gone, thin flakes like frost on the ground appeared on the desert floor. When the Israelites saw it, they said to each other, 'What is it?' For they did not know what it was.
>
> Moses said to them, 'It is the bread the LORD has given you to eat. This is what the LORD has commanded: "Everyone is to gather as much as they need. Take an omer [about 1.5 kilos or 3 pounds] for each person you have in your tent."'
>
> The Israelites did as they were told; some gathered much, some little. And when they measured it by the omer, the one who gathered much did not have too much, and the one who gathered little did not have too little. Everyone had gathered just as much as they needed.
>
> Then Moses said to them, 'No one is to keep any of it until morning.'
>
> However, some of them paid no attention to Moses; they kept part of it until morning, but it was full of maggots and began to smell. So Moses was angry with them.
>
> Each morning everyone gathered as much as they needed, and when the sun grew hot, it melted away (Exodus 16:13–21).

Think carefully about this special daily bread from heaven. The Lord provided *plenty* for every person for each and every day. Whatever people gathered was enough to sustain them for the whole day. He faithfully provided daily bread without fail, every day for the forty years God's people were in that wilderness. Some people tried to gather more of this daily bread, storing it up for the next day. Why would they do that? Some obviously didn't trust that there would be bread the next day. They wanted to get some security. They were worrying about the needs of tomorrow right now, today. They wanted to have treasure and resources stored up for the future. When they did that, the daily bread they stored up 'was full of maggots and began to smell'. This special daily bread from the Lord had a very limited life span. It melted away every morning as the sun grew hot, and if anybody tried to keep it overnight it literally became rotten.

The Lord was teaching His people a deep lesson about our daily life. He gives us what we need for today, but we cannot store up what He gives us today for tomorrow. In other words, we need to come to Him every single day for help. We cannot go even one day without coming to Him for help. We can't have one long prayer at the beginning of the week, to cover all the days of the week, or just read fifty chapters of the Bible once a month. No! We follow the Lord Jesus *one day at a time*. This really is one of the big themes of the Bible. We must start every day with prayer and Bible reading. Every day we must draw near to the Lord God. Every day we must repent, turning from our sin and towards the Lord Jesus. Every day we must take time to chew over the Word of God, taking it down into our hearts, letting it shape our minds. It is the daily practice of prayer and Bible study that captures our hearts and minds for the Living God, keeping depression away from us, making sure we are thinking in the right way and able to reject the lies of the devil. Every day we must begin again. Every day we must trust Him; every day we must listen to His voice; every day we must not harden our hearts; every day we must come to Him for the help we need to get through that day.

The basic unit of time for the Living God is the day. He doesn't think primarily in terms of months, years, decades or millennia—but simply in terms of *days*. Yes, He is infinite and sees the whole of time, from eternity past right through to an eternal future, but His basic way of dealing with us is in terms of one day at a time. The issue before us is not what happened yesterday, because no matter how much we may feel trapped and defined by the past, He can cleanse us, forgive us, heal us and resurrect us. *Yesterday* can be defeated by the power of Jesus' death and resurrection. *Tomorrow* is beyond us. We do not know if we will be alive tomorrow, and we do not know what will happen. Our heavenly Father holds the future and He alone has power to determine what happens tomorrow. He has forbidden us from *worrying* about tomorrow. Yes, we can make wise preparation for tomorrow, but we must never *worry* about tomorrow. He designed us to cope with just one day at a time. We might think we have the ability to plan and organize many days all at once in our calendars and planning software, but it is a deceitful illusion. We can make tentative plans, but we must live with a deep awareness that we do not control tomorrow. We can only look to the will of the Father when we put dates in our diaries. If we are going to live with peace and purpose, we must manage only one day at a time.

Our daily bread is the Lord Jesus Himself. He called Himself the Bread of Life, and until we eat of that food each day we will never really *live*. Every day we need to come to the Bread of Life for our daily bread. Thomas Fuller said that we do not know if we will be given any more days, so we dare not postpone our repenting until tomorrow. How many millions of people died with the intention of doing business with God 'soon', 'in the future', 'when I'm ready', 'when I get on top of things'. Jesus told the story of a man who was doing well in life. He went to bed one night full of bright plans for the future. He thought that the main item on his agenda for the next day was to build more storage for all his possessions. Yet that very night his soul was required of him and he died. He died in utter spiritual poverty, doomed to be lost in the vast empty darkness of eternity, shut out from life and light for ever. He thought that he needed to deal with the business of *this* life, but his time had run out. He never got round to the only business that really mattered: the business of eternity; his business with the Living God in Jesus (Luke 12:13–21).

The point is this: our main business every day is to receive our daily bread from Jesus, the Bread of Life. Our daily bread is much more than the physical needs of our bodies: our food, water and clothing. Our heavenly Father knows all about these bodily needs and He will provide for them, if we first hunger and thirst for His kingdom and His righteousness.

In the Lord's prayer we have just prayed for His kingdom to come and His will to be done; now we come with empty hands asking for help. We wait on the Lord every day to renew our strength: to see properly; to hear what needs to be heard; to find the eternal life we need to get through *this* day.

# Reflections

## ASR Roddy MacLeod

I was helping a young recruit who had broken his ankle during training and was feeling pretty low and discouraged. He is a committed Christian but kept talking about the 'what if's that life might hold for him in the coming days. He was in Sword Company, which is a rehab unit that allows you some time to recover. If you don't recover fairly quickly you are discharged out of the army. I spent many days encouraging this young soldier to deal with one day at a time and leave all the 'what if's to God, who is more than capable. It was great to see how this Christian man enjoyed and valued both meeting up to pray and studying the Bible. He did get better and finished his training—and he learned that God provides, each day at a time.

## ASR Lee McDade

It has been said that 'an army marches on its stomach' and 'a happy soldier is a soldier who is fed, watered and rested'. It's one of the reasons why, when I visit troops in the field, I always take a bag of chocolate bars or sweets with me; not to do so would be criminal! Sweets and chocolate bars are not the only sustenance I like to share with soldiers: I love to share the Word of God. I have the privilege of doing so in a couple of different ways. It has been my pleasure to give out thousands of New Testaments and Psalms over the last few years at our church parades and to share some words of encouragement from them, including 'For God so loved the world that he gave his one and only Son, that whoever believes in him shall not perish but have eternal life' (John 3:16). It's a joy to share such nourishment with sometimes 200 soldiers at a time, knowing that His Word never comes back void; it accomplishes all it needs to. I encourage soldiers to read and taste the Scriptures for themselves. I have had many young men tell me they have read the Bible they received at that initial service. There are also great opportunities to share God's Word with the troops in the field in the camp, even in smoking shelters. I love encouraging troops through God's Word, and hearing feedback from them on how much it has meant to them, especially when they have been wet, tired or low in energy. Proverbs 16:24 says this: 'Gracious words are a honeycomb, sweet to the soul and healing to the bones.' This is a verse I have seen in action while sharing the Word with soldiers. I get to offer them a different type of bread: not fried or toasted but everlasting and imperishable. It's been an honour over the last few years to give out New Testaments, full Bibles and many copies of *Our Daily Bread* devotionals. Taste and see that the Lord is good!

## ASR Gavin Dickson

Each day I face at least 600 soldiers with a message that is not widely respected. I walk through the gates of an army camp that houses, trains and equips soldiers to fight our nation's wars. I go to tell them they need Jesus and they need to be saved. Each day I do this, I need daily bread to sustain me. Each day I need to read God's Word and I need to pray, or I will not be useful and will not find the courage to walk into the camp, let alone talk to the men and women of our Armed Forces, in their own environment, about the wonderful gospel message.

## ASR & Area Rep Paul Somerville

Entering the RAF accommodation I met an SAC (Senior Aircraftman) in the corridor and he asked if he could become a Christian! We sat down and I asked why. He said, 'Because I am representing my unit in a boxing match and I have been told that, if I have God in my corner, I'll win!' I opened my Bible and showed him from Romans why we need God, and how we can know God through His Son Jesus. The young lad had never heard this before, but he listened, and having heard the 'bad news' about his motives he then heard the 'good news' of the gospel. In his little barracks room he trusted the Lord, not as some good-luck charm, but as his Saviour, the great sin-bearer. Did he win his fight? Well, that's another story!

## ASR Paul Curd

It is the most wonderful feeling in the world to know that God 'has your back'. In our flesh we can fret and worry about the most trivial of things—and the most important of things. Of course to us, in our humanity, almost everything seems important. Thankfully, God knows the bigger picture! I found this to be true especially when we were moving house so that I could take up the post of Scripture Reader in Pirbright. Financially, we didn't have the means for all we needed. But I decided that if God had called me to this work, then ensuring we had all that we needed was something I needn't concern myself with. And through various means we were able to obtain everything we needed! It is the most freeing thing in the world to simply trust God, especially when something seems impossible. Hardships can teach us many things, not least of which is how to trust Him.

Of course, having our daily needs supplied is only part of 'our daily bread'! I have a big box full of *Our Daily Bread* Volume 3 devotional booklets, with a whole year of readings especially selected for soldiers. They have a neat combat design and the recruits love to receive one. As I once handed a few out to a small group of interested recruits after the chapel service I was asked what was meant by 'Daily

Bread'. I responded by asking them what they had had for lunch on a particular day a week beforehand. Of course they couldn't remember, so I explained that for the Christian it is the same: just as some meals are more memorable than others, but all have done their job of keeping us alive, so, when we read them, some Scriptures are more poignant than others, but all have done their job of keeping us 'spiritually' alive! They understood the concept immediately and went on to ask more about the Bible itself. What an amazing privilege, and responsibility, to be able to explain these things to some from a largely unchurched generation. I pray that recruits who have received a copy of *Our Daily Bread* might have an encounter with the Bread of Life, our Lord and Saviour.

### ASR Meg Atkinson

While walking around my barracks I came across a group of soldiers stood in rank and file awaiting instruction. When I asked the soldier in charge if the boys had time to enjoy some food for the body, the parade descended into chaos. Soon order was restored, but as I walked to my car a young soldier followed, asking if I had any more little booklets on daily thoughts. I had given him one once before. Here was a young man who knew my chocolate bars were no match for the Bread of heaven!

# 7. Forgive us our sins, as we forgive those who sin against us

Right at the heart of the Lord's Prayer is a simple request: 'forgive us our sins'. That is the prayer that lies at the very heart of life itself: until we openly acknowledge that we are a mess in the eyes of the Living God and that we need His forgiveness, we haven't understood what this life is all about. As long as we are trying to fix our own lives or earn the approval of God (or of anybody else) we are slaves, doomed to darkness not only in this life but for all eternity. If we will not truly and openly ask for forgiveness each day it means that we do not understand either what a mess we make each day or why Jesus and His death is the centre of the universe and history.

The Bible is full of blood sacrifice, from the first book to the last book. Altars are built and animals are sacrificed for thousands of years all the way through the Old Testament, and even right at the end of the Bible, when we look into the heart of heaven, we see God Himself as a lamb that has been sacrificed. Until we really understand and *love* the heart of *this* we do not know the Living God. Many people are even *embarrassed* by all this blood and sacrifice, as if it were some kind of barbaric and primitive superstition. Such people have tried to explain it away and say that the only message God has is that He loves us all. It is true that He loves us all with a jealous and passionate love, but that is not all He has to say to us. He is also deeply angered by the way we live and by what we desire and the things we say. He is disgusted by the lifestyles we love to lead and He *cannot* have anything to do with us as long as we are bound to these things. He loves us, yes, but it is precisely because He takes us so seriously that He will not ignore us and simply shrug His shoulders about the things we have done and the state of our hearts. He takes us all with total and eternal seriousness, treating us as the kings and queens of creation that He designed us to be. What we have done and thought and desired; what we have fantasized about; what we have said; all the things we have failed to do; the needs we have ignored; the laziness and cowardice we have indulged: all this must be confronted and dealt with. We might wish it could all just be ignored and forgotten, that we could just please ourselves or even try to fix ourselves; but this holy and glorious God will always address all the darkness, all the mess, all the sin. He holds us accountable for all we have ever done or said, all we have ever thought or imagined—not because He hates us; not because He is a tyrant; but because He takes us more seriously than we could ever dream. He will go to any lengths to make us right with Him, to heal us from all the things we have done wrong, to teach us how to find true, eternal life. There is no limit to what the Living God will do for you to cleanse you from your shame and selfishness, to give you a new beginning, to keep you with Him, in His family, for ever and ever.

I once heard about a man who drowned because he had fallen through some ice and it was too dangerous for anybody to try to help him. Even the rescue services wouldn't risk their own safety to get to him. Yet the Living God did not hesitate when it was time to rescue us. The Living God became a human being and ended up jumping right into the worst of our mess and darkness, caring nothing for His own safety. He lost His own life; broke His own heart; shed His own blood; and refused to turn back, even when He was as cursed, filthy and dying as the worst of us. He will never turn back, no matter the cost to Himself, if we call to Him for help. We know this for sure because the immortal God went to a cursed death, a God-forsaken death! If He did that to make it possible to drag us out of our mess and bring us into His family for ever and ever, going down to the very bottom of the deepest pit, into the very darkest darkness, to find the very worst of us, we know that there is nothing He will not do to confront our sin and save us from its guilt, its shame and its power.

We need to consider this carefully to understand how important it is for us to pray these few words with heartfelt seriousness every day: 'forgive us our sins.' We pray those words, and we come back to the central reality in all the heavens and the earth: the Lord Jesus who died for us to take away our sins. In humility and trust, in brokenness and love, we come back to Him as our only hope and our only Saviour every single day. Yet, with our hearts and minds fixed only on *Him*, the Lord's Prayer immediately sends us back to consider how we should reflect that forgiveness to other people. *We are immediately tested to see whether this forgiveness from the Father has really reached us.* In fact, in Matthew 6:14–15 Jesus immediately gives a further emphasis to this part of the prayer, underlining that He really did mean what He said:

> For if you forgive other people when they sin against
> you, your heavenly Father will also forgive you. But if
> you do not forgive others their sins, your Father will not
> forgive your sins.

So vital is it for us to understand this as Jesus intended that we need to go to Matthew 18:21–35, where Jesus, provoked by Peter, very specifically spelled it out in a parable:

> Peter came to Jesus and asked, 'Lord, how many times
> shall I forgive my brother or sister who sins against me?
> Up to seven times?'

> Jesus answered, 'I tell you, not seven times, but seventy-
> seven times.

> 'Therefore, the kingdom of heaven is like a king who
> wanted to settle accounts with his servants. As he began
> the settlement, a man who owed him ten thousand bags
> of gold [or talents] was brought to him. Since he was
> not able to pay, the master ordered that he and his wife
> and his children and all that he had be sold to repay
> the debt.

> 'At this the servant fell on his knees before him. "Be
> patient with me," he begged, "and I will pay back
> everything." The servant's master took pity on him,
> cancelled the debt and let him go.

> 'But when that servant went out, he found one of his
> fellow servants who owed him a hundred silver coins
> [or denarii]. He grabbed him and began to choke him.
> "Pay back what you owe me!" he demanded.

> 'His fellow servant fell to his knees and begged him,
> "Be patient with me, and I will pay it back."

'But he refused. Instead, he went off and had the man thrown into prison until he could pay the debt. When the other servants saw what had happened, they were outraged and went and told their master everything that had happened.

'Then the master called the servant in. "You wicked servant," he said, "I cancelled all that debt of yours because you begged me to. Shouldn't you have had mercy on your fellow servant just as I had on you?" In anger his master handed him over to the jailers to be tortured, until he should pay back all he owed.

'This is how my heavenly Father will treat each of you unless you forgive your brother or sister from your heart.'

Peter's question has some important details. First, Peter knows that he must forgive, but he wants to know how many times he has to keep on doing this. This is important. Peter is already miles further on than some who don't really want to forgive at all. Many people hold grudges and can remember things said or done to them from many years ago. Well, Peter is not like that; he knows that forgiveness is an essential aspect of Christian life.

Second, Peter is thinking especially of the forgiveness given to 'my brother or sister', someone in God's family. This is the very hardest kind of forgiveness to give so Peter perhaps starts with the hardest case. When a stranger or 'outsider' offends us, the pain is real, but it never bites so deeply and bitterly as when a friend or church family member hurts us. If we are betrayed, let down or offended by our brothers and sisters in the local church family, it can go very deep, and forgiveness might be much harder and more costly to give.

Third, Peter sets the bar quite high. He has obviously been thinking hard about this and he can see how vital forgiveness really is. It is not enough to forgive just once or twice, especially within the church family. So what if we were to show forgiveness and healing *seven* times, no matter how hard that might be? Peter perhaps thought he might even impress Jesus: Did Jesus think it might be necessary to forgive *even up to seven times*?!

When Jesus answered it must have sounded ridiculous and impossible: '*I tell you, not seven times, but seventy-seven times.*' It is possible that Jesus even said 'seventy times seven times'—taking us up to nearly 500 repetitions of forgiveness! The point is clear if not outrageous: *there can be no limit to forgiveness.* There is no time when a grudge or bitterness is the right course of action. There is *never* a time when we throw the weight and responsibility back onto the offender rather than holding out true forgiveness. If we are offended by anybody, we need to go and offer our hand, in love and grace—and *always* offer our hand in love and grace. We must always say 'hello' with warmth and always pray for blessing on those who have offended us, and bring them whatever blessing we can. That is how to change them, to win them, to break their hard hearts, according to the Bible. At first this seems impossible and unreasonable, so Jesus tells this story to show us what is really at stake. The way we forgive others flows out of our salvation, *from the way we have been forgiven.* If we do *not* forgive, or if we are limited or grudging in our forgiveness, it reveals either that we have not yet been forgiven or that perhaps we have not understood our forgiveness.

> The kingdom of heaven is like a king who wanted
> to settle accounts with his servants. As he began the
> settlement, a man who owed him ten thousand bags of
> gold [or talents] was brought to him.

A talent was a lot of money; some estimate that it was equivalent to ten to twenty years of labour for a manual worker. It was equivalent to at least £100,000 in today's terms. So ten thousand talents would be equivalent to £1 billion at the very least! How on earth had this man got into such levels of debt to this king?

> Since he was not able to pay, the master ordered that he,
> his wife, his children and all that he had be sold to repay
> the debt.

This might sound quite harsh treatment at first, but when we realize the amount of money involved it seems much more reasonable. No king could write off that much money, and he needed to try to claw back whatever he could on this huge debt.

> The servant fell on his knees before him. 'Be patient
> with me,' he begged, 'and I will pay back everything.'

Now this is ridiculous! No matter how patient the king was, he was never going to get his £1 billion back from this man and his family. It's the sort of thing we might say when we are praying about our sins: 'Heavenly Father, I'm so very sorry for what I've done. Please be merciful to me and forgive me, *and I promise I will never do it, or any other sins, ever again.*' Our heavenly Father will never show us mercy on the basis of such a promise! If He were only to forgive us if we could repay our debt or if we could guarantee no further sins, none of us could ever be forgiven! No: just like the king in the story, our heavenly

Father forgives us knowing full well that we can neither repay Him nor guarantee no further debts.

> The servant's master took pity on him, cancelled the debt and let him go.

Think about what this meant for the king. He had to run his country and he carried all kinds of heavy responsibilities. He really needed that £1 billion for his own work and care. Yet he took the burden of that massive debt onto himself. *Someone* had to carry the weight of that debt; it couldn't just disappear. It wasn't just numbers on a piece of paper! So that king took that debt onto himself, and he would have had to find a way to make that back in some other way.

That was how it was at the cross when Christ took the cost of our debt on Himself. The forgiveness is utterly free *to us*, but it was frighteningly costly *to Him*.

> But when that servant went out, he found one of his fellow servants who owed him a hundred silver coins [or denarii]. He grabbed him and began to choke him. 'Pay back what you owe me!' he demanded.

A denarius was a day's pay for a manual labourer in the Roman empire, probably equivalent to around £10–15 in today's terms. So 100 denarii might have been somewhere between £1,000 and £2,000. This was not just a few coppers or mere pocket money; it was a sizeable amount of money—but compared with the £1 billion, it was very small indeed.

Can you see the point? Judged on its own—out of context—a debt of £1,000 seems very large. It is too much to write off and forget. However, when placed next to a debt of £1 billion, it suddenly seems very small indeed.

One debt is literally a million times bigger than the other! So how would this man react to the fact that someone owed him £1,000?

> His fellow servant fell to his knees and begged him, 'Be patient with me, and I will pay you back.' But he refused. Instead, he went off and had the man thrown into prison until he could pay the debt.

First, this reveals something of how this man thought about money. Maybe his greed for money had got him into the £1 billion of debt in the first place. The king clearly valued *people* much more highly than *money*. He saw that man and his family as being worth more than £1 billion and was prepared to forget the £1 billion in order to give this man and his family life. But this man could not see the treasure of the new beginning he had been given. He had been set free from a terrible, immovable, crushing debt—*yet he was still in chains*, still crushed under a burden of greed and selfishness. He had no *life*. The forgiveness had been given to him, but *he had not received it*. The man was still bound up in grasping and selfishness. He was still locked into an attitude that feels it should get what it deserves. He was still trying to be a judge over others. The other servants immediately realized that something very wrong and sick was going on. How could one who had been forgiven so much be so harsh in his own forgiveness?

> The master called the servant in. 'You wicked servant,' he said, 'I cancelled all that debt of yours because you begged me to. Shouldn't you have had mercy on your fellow servant just as I had on you?' In anger his master turned him over to the jailers to be tortured, until he should pay back all he owed.

Having told this parable, Jesus makes the following conclusion, which gets right to the heart of it all:

> This is how my heavenly Father will treat each of you unless you forgive your brother or sister from your heart.

God's free forgiveness is offered to us—all our debts have been paid at the cross. However, we can see right away whether a person has ever received and really *experienced* that gracious forgiveness by the way he or she treats and forgives other people. Every time somebody hurts us, offends us or speaks against one of our friends or family members: How do we react to that? How do we respond? *That* reveals where we stand with our heavenly Father. So deep and essential is this truth that Jesus wants us to pray about it every single day: 'Forgive us our sins, *as we forgive those who sin against us.*'

This is deep and challenging. If we don't really understand this level of forgiveness, it is very likely that we have never been forgiven: we are not yet Christians. We need to listen to this warning and seek that full and free forgiveness that the Father will give if we turn round and kneel before Him. This is where we face the deep challenges of our hearts, of the way we live: of what really matters to us. Forgiveness is at the very centre of true life. If we do not know how to forgive, we can be sure we have never been forgiven. Nothing in life is more serious than this. Every single day we must keep short accounts with the Living God and also with each other. Every day we must genuinely seek forgiveness from Him and seek to show forgiveness to one another.

# Reflections

## ASR Ken Surgenor

I led the prayers at our recent
Remembrance Service on camp,
concluding with the Lord's Prayer.
After the service I was approached by a CSM, who
asked me, 'Why do you say "Forgive us our trespasses,
as we forgive those who trespass against us" when I
say "Forgive us our debts, as we forgive our debtors"?'
I told him that he was correctly quoting Matthew 6:12
in the Authorized Version of the Bible, but that the
main thing was that 'debts' or 'trespasses' means the
same thing: sin. And though we can forgive those who
wrong us or hurt us, we cannot forgive them their
sins. There is only One who can forgive sins: the Lord
Jesus Christ, who paid the price at Calvary for all our
sin, so that we might be reconciled to God. John 14:6:
'Jesus saith unto him, I am the way, the truth, and
the life: no man cometh unto the Father, but by me'
(KJV). The CSM smiled at me. I trust that God will be
the centre of every conversation of ours, and that the
Holy Spirit will work in the CSM.

## ASR Nick Wilson

I was always emphasizing the importance of forgiveness during my time at Pirbright. Once when there were twenty recruits in a Padre's Hour I asked if anyone came from a broken home. Nineteen out of the twenty put up their hands: many harboured hatred towards their parents, usually for having left them. I explained to them that the only reason why I knew true joy instead of hatred or anger was because I had been able to forgive everyone who had hurt me deeply, because Christ had forgiven me. I chose Christ many years ago. My first wife left because of my decision to follow Him, and both my parents disinherited me. I stressed to the recruits that, nevertheless, I could not be eaten up by hatred because of Christ's love and forgiveness towards me.

A lovely lad called William, who had not seen his dad for ten years, said, 'Nick, you are always preaching on forgiveness; what should I do?' 'Give your dad a ring,' I suggested. He came to see me a week later: 'I'm going to see my dad next weekend, half way through basic training!' They got on so well together that he planned to spend his next leave with his dad at the end of basic training! He was reconciled not only to his earthly father, but also to his heavenly Father! He chose Christ, experienced His forgiveness, and committed himself to following Him. I went home crying with joy that day, that my heavenly Father had seen fit to use me in this way.

## ASR Ray Hendricks

I was directed to a soldier who had been tried in court and was awaiting his sentence. He was so ashamed that he was contemplating suicide. My first act was to assure the young man that I did not judge him. The second was to explain that if he was truly sorry for his actions, the first person to know that was the Lord Jesus Christ. The Bible says that He searches our hearts to know the truth.

I told him the Bible story of the woman caught in the act of adultery who was brought before Jesus (John 8). I told the soldier to note what Jesus said to the woman: because He was able to tell that she was truly repentant (sorry enough to want never to do that deed again), He forgave her of her sins. But I also told the soldier to notice the warning He gave her: to sin no more.

This young man said he was truly sorry and he would never again do anything like this. I encouraged him to confess to Jesus Christ. He did this by praying his own prayer in my presence—and he accepted a Bible. His demeanour changed from depression to hope! For the remaining nine days of his stay in the detention facility he read his Bible and welcomed me talking about it. It is my hope that he will continue with the Lord, regardless of the difficulties of being in a civilian prison.

## ASR & Area Rep Steve Penny

As an evangelistic outreach,
some serving SASRA members
had invited a number of young
soldiers from the local barracks
to join Christians from a local
church for a meal in a restaurant
and to hear some testimonies. The group heard the
testimony of one soldier who had recently become a
Christian. He shared how he had been overwhelmed
by the love of God, and that the knowledge of this
was key to his seeking Christ. The soldiers then
heard a second testimony describing how we need to
ask for forgiveness for the wrong we have all done,
for 'all have sinned and fall short of the glory of
God' (Romans 3:23), but 'If we confess our sins, he
is faithful and just and will forgive us our sins and
purify us from all unrighteousness' (1 John 1:9). It
is important for soldiers considering faith in Christ to
understand God's nature as being both love and justice.

## ASR Meg Atkinson

During my regular Friday evening visit to the WRAF block, I got into conversation with Bev. We were both very sporty and our various activities were our main subject of conversation. I would talk about Jesus in a natural way within the context of my activities. One evening, after our sporty chat, Bev asked if I could tell her how to be confirmed. 'Why do you want to be confirmed?' I enquired. 'I'd love to know Jesus like you,' she replied. I told Bev I hadn't been confirmed but converted. I opened my Bible at Matthew 18:3. After I had unpacked what the verse meant, we got on our knees and prayed, and Bev surrendered to the Saviour and experienced her sins forgiven for the first time. Bev went on to marry and, some thirty years later, is in full-time ministry.

# 8. Lead us not into temptation, but deliver us from the evil one

Our studies in the Lord's Prayer began in the heights of heaven with the Father and they end with sin, temptation and the devil: 'lead us not into temptation, but deliver us from the evil one'. If this is to be prayed properly it must be prayed with desperation and urgency. If we do not know how vulnerable we are, how urgently we need to be protected from temptation and trial, we will not understand this concluding prayer. If we are busy trying to stop sin in our lives by trying harder or by being more disciplined, *we are deluded*.

Our flesh is weak and our natural hearts are deceitful and desperately wicked. From that perspective, sin and the devil own us. If I go to war against sin and the devil in the strength of my flesh, I am defeated. I will live a life of frustration, guilt and shame. Yes, I may get on top of a few superficial bad habits, but the deepest issues lie too deep. I may obsess about the obvious addictions and surface-level sins, but I am usually almost completely blind to the deepest corruption of my flesh. So, if we are going to pray this last part of the Lord's Prayer, we need to be deeply aware of the desperate mess we are in. As long as I think I need only a bit of help and encouragement, I will never pray this prayer properly.

Let's begin right there. How important is this prayer? Why do we need to pray this? The fact that Jesus was able to withstand the devil for three temptations is one of the greatest marvels in all the biographies of His life. It is a wonder and a miracle of staggering proportions. The devil had never before met a man who could withstand him. Notice that the Lord's Prayer asks that we might never even face temptation, as if we are frightened of our ability to withstand it. Do we pray like that? Or do we suspect that as long as we get a bit of encouragement we will be able to go into temptation and face the devil?

The book of Job gives us a more detailed example of the devil asking to sift someone. It is an incredible book that shows us how the devil works. The book begins with this strange situation of the devil requesting permission to test Job. The devil always suspects that people follow the Lord only because they are paid to do so. The devil assumes that everybody acts out of simple self-interest; that in the end, everybody is controlled by the flesh, by personal desires. When he sees that someone is following Jesus, the devil will sooner or later want to test that commitment. He will want to sift that person and find out how strong that commitment really is. We must never underestimate this tempting power of the devil, together with the answering darkness of our own hearts. *The devil has such power because he tells us what we want to hear, what the flesh longs for.* If any of us imagine for one moment that we can withstand the power of the devil, we are frighteningly deluded. The whole book of Job moves to a concluding section when the Lord God appears to Job and explains all the wonders He can do in the creation and management of the whole created order, from ruling over the oceans to organizing all the stars and the galaxies. As the Living God describes the sheer glorious extent of His power and wisdom, He reaches a mighty final crescendo in chapter 41, when he reveals the thing He can do that should really humble Job *more than anything else*. The final claim of the Lord God is that He alone can defeat Leviathan:

> Can you pull in Leviathan with a fishhook
>> or tie down its tongue with a rope? ...
> If you lay a hand on it,
>> you will remember the struggle and never do it again!
> Any hope of subduing it is false;
>> the mere sight of it is overpowering.
> No one is fierce enough to rouse it.
>> Who then is able to stand against me?
> Who has a claim against me that I must pay?
>> Everything under heaven belongs to me.
> I will not fail to speak of Leviathan's limbs,
>> its strength and its graceful form.
> Who can strip off its outer coat?
>> Who can penetrate its double coat of armour?
> Who dares open the doors of its mouth,
>> ringed about with its fearsome teeth? ...
> Its snorting throws out flashes of light;
>> its eyes are like the rays of dawn.
> Flames stream from its mouth;
>> sparks of fire shoot out.
> Smoke pours from its nostrils
>> as from a boiling pot over burning reeds.
> Its breath sets coals ablaze,
>> and flames dart from its mouth ...
> The sword that reaches it has no effect,
>> nor does the spear or the dart or the javelin ...
> Nothing on earth is its equal—
>> a creature without fear.

It looks down on all that are haughty;
it is king over all that are proud

(Job 41:1, 8–14, 18–21, 26, 33–34).

Job 41 warns us that we cannot defeat this greatest of all creatures, this mighty dragon who breathes fire and is invincible against all human weapons. The book of Job began with the devil causing mayhem, and throughout the book we are worried about this mighty dragon that is able to cause such suffering and evil on the earth. It is only in the climactic final chapters that we hear that there is a heavenly Champion who is able to make the mighty dragon beg for mercy. Whenever I want to have a fresh appreciation of why every day I need to pray 'deliver me from the evil one', I read Job 41. This mighty and terrible dragon that lives in the ocean of the abyss is more than a match for us. If he comes to tempt us, we are in serious trouble. Each day, more than once, we need to pray, 'lead us not into temptation, but deliver us from the evil one.'

In an age of self-reliance we need constant reminders of this. We are filled with an inflated sense of our own abilities, especially in spiritual matters, so this prayer will not come naturally to us. Even if we call ourselves followers of Jesus, we might well pass over this final part of the Lord's prayer as if it were a mere formality, as if as long as we vaguely trust Jesus we will be in no real danger from temptation or the devil. Some Christians speak too flippantly about the devil and his armies. They say that as long as we belong to Jesus and are filled with the Spirit, the devil can't touch us. Yes, that is true; but it is only true if we are really finding our refuge in Jesus and are daily filled with the Spirit. The Bible shows us many examples of the very best Christians who forgot to run to Jesus and be filled with the Spirit. Remember how, in Matthew 16, Peter had just declared that Jesus was the Christ, the Son of God, and Jesus had told Peter that this truth had been given to him by the Father in heaven (v. 17). Surely Peter was safe from the devil's influence at that time! Peter had been the mouthpiece for the Father's wisdom, so how could the devil ever touch him? Jesus then began to teach the disciples about the need for the cross: how He had to suffer and die to save us. Even as Jesus was speaking about this most important subject Peter let his guard down and began to rely on his own flesh. He grieved the Spirit when he began to reject Jesus' teaching of the cross; he actually dared to rebuke Jesus and tell Him to stay away from the cross. When Peter spoke like that Jesus said to Peter, 'Get behind me, Satan!' (v. 23).

Think about that for a moment. Peter spoke words straight from the Father—wonderful words of truth and life. Then a few minutes later Peter spoke words straight from Satan—terrible words of unbelief and selfishness. The moment Peter stopped trusting Jesus and walking in the Spirit, he was open to the influence and temptations of the devil. Peter had fallen from the highest spiritual experience to the deepest darkness of the devil, all in a few minutes.

You may have experienced this in your own life. You may have had a wonderful spiritual time at church and really felt the reality of the Living God. Then you go home, and within a short time you are wallowing in sinful sewage, utterly caught in the darkness and evil of sin. How can this happen? How can we so easily fall under the influence of the devil? In our own strength we are owned by the devil and sin. Our own flesh cannot do anything good at all, and until we deeply appreciate this we will never pray this prayer as we should. That is the reality behind this part of the Lord's Prayer. In the Garden of Gethsemane, Jesus Himself was praying with terrible desperation and urgency. It was this part of His daily pattern of prayer that He was urging on His closest friends. Remember what Jesus said to His disciples at that time of testing when He returned to them and found them sleeping: '"Couldn't you men keep watch with me for one hour?" he asked Peter. "Watch and pray so that you will not fall into temptation. The spirit is willing, but the flesh is weak"' (Matthew 26:40–41).

The disciples were complacent. They didn't realize how weak their flesh really was. They assumed that they were strong enough to withstand temptation, to handle any sifting that the devil threw at them. They were also very tired and assumed *that prayer could wait*; that Jesus was overreacting; that a good night's sleep was the best preparation for a challenging day. Jesus knew better, and when the hour of darkness came He was ready to act in a perfect, godly and courageous way. The disciples had failed to pray this final part of the Lord's Prayer and they fell to pieces. Peter turned to violence and later denial, while the other disciples simply ran away.

The evil one is the temptation specialist. He tries different strategies. In the case of Job, who had so much ease and comfort, the devil wanted to see how he would cope with the loss of the Lord's blessings. Would Job still follow the Lord if the temporal blessings of this life were taken away?

If we go back to Eve at the beginning of the world, he simply got her to think about her own self-interest. Didn't she want to be like God? Wouldn't it be better for her to get more knowledge, to improve herself? Wasn't the Living God trying to keep some real benefits from her? In Peter's first letter, he warns us how the devil will try to make us desire an easy, comfortable, popular life rather than the sacrificial life of suffering, self-denial and loving service that Jesus gives us. Peter knew what it was to be influenced by the devil. He knew the temptation to try to keep hold of a life of comfort and safety, of health and wealth, rather than following Jesus in the way of the cross. Listen to Peter's warning about the devil from 1 Peter 5:

> Humble yourselves, therefore, under God's mighty hand, that he may lift you up in due time. Cast all your anxiety on him because he cares for you.
>
> Be alert and of sober mind. Your enemy the devil prowls around like a roaring lion looking for someone to devour. Resist him, standing firm in the faith, because you know that the family of believers throughout the world is undergoing the same kind of sufferings.
>
> And the God of all grace, who called you to his eternal glory in Christ, after you have suffered a little while, will himself restore you and make you strong, firm and steadfast. To him be the power for ever and ever. Amen (1 Peter 5:6–11).

The devil might bring us suffering, but it is more likely that he will make us so *afraid* of suffering, poverty or illness that we abandon Jesus to save ourselves. The devil will try to persuade us that it is too hard to follow Jesus or that Jesus has brought too much hardship upon us. He will tempt us to think that we should reject the cross and try to grasp the comforts of the flesh and the world. The devil will find our weakness and constantly exploit it. He may leave us alone in some areas if he knows that he *owns* us in another area. He may never need to tempt us in the area of compassion or laziness because he knows that we will always listen to him in the area of anger, lust or greed.

This concluding part of the Lord's Prayer takes us into the very depths of reality. As long as we think we can save ourselves from our own sin by trying harder, we are doomed. Let me repeat that because it is so desperately important: *As long as we think we can save ourselves or fix our problems by trying harder, we are doomed.* The follower of Jesus, the one who has a *living* relationship with the Living God, is the one who kneels before Him and says, 'Save me! I cannot save myself. My sin and my sinful heart are too strong for me. The devil has devoured me and *I can never overcome that mighty dragon.* Please have mercy on me! In the Name of Jesus the Saviour, save me! Deliver me from the evil one!'

Peter learned the hard way how desperately important that final part of the Lord's prayer is. He failed in the Garden when he should have been praying. However, as we read in 1 Peter 5, later in his life he wanted us all to know that we need humbly to submit ourselves to the power of God, facing whatever suffering and hardship may come, trusting that only our gracious God can lift us up.

The Lord's Prayer is not just something to be recited each day when we are tired or distressed; it is wonderfully comforting to use this simple prayer. Jesus was giving us the basic *pattern* of prayer, a structure to guide us into as much prayer as we want. We open out these clauses and expand the truths and requests that are in them. Perhaps we might spend a whole morning simply meditating and praying over the Father in heaven and His holy Name; or we might need to spend much time finding forgiveness in our hearts for terrible wrong done to us. We might feel especially weak in the face of temptation or defeated by the devil. In all these circumstances we open up those parts of the pattern of prayer and speak to our heavenly Father through the Name of Jesus, in the power of the Spirit. The key to everything is that we pray. If we don't pray it is because we think we don't need to. *In our urgent needs, we all turn to prayer—but when we don't pray it is because we don't see our urgent need for the Living God each and every day.* Perhaps we fear that our prayers are not really heard, that nothing changes through prayer. Perhaps we fear that prayer changes our own minds but can never change the mind of God.

We end with these words from the great Baptist preacher Charles Spurgeon, preaching on Jeremiah 33:3: 'Call to me and I will answer you and tell you great and unsearchable things you do not know.'

> God encourages us to *pray*. Our enemies tell us that *prayer* is a pious exercise which has no influence. We know better. Our experience gives the lie a thousand times over to this infidel assertion. Here the living God distinctly promises to answer *prayer*. Let us *call upon* Him again and allow no doubts about Him hearing us and answering us. He that made the ear, shall He not hear? He that gave parents a love to their children, will He not listen to the cries of His own sons and daughters? God will answer His *pleading* people in their anguish. He has wonders in store for them. What they

have never seen, heard of, or dreamed of, He will do for them. He will invent new blessings if needful. He will ransack sea and land to feed them: He will send every angel out of heaven to help them, if their distress requires it. He will astound us with His grace and make us feel that it was never before done in this fashion. All He asks of us is that we will *call upon* Him.[3]

3  Charles Spurgeon, *Faith's Check Book*, meditation for 29 June, http://www.ccel.org/ccel/spurgeon/checkbook.viii.html.

# Reflections

## ASR William Wade

As a young soldier serving in
Germany in the early 1990s, I
was trying to maintain a strong
Christian witness to the regiment I was serving
with: the Royal Irish Rangers. This testimony was
challenged very early one Saturday morning as I
was roughly shaken out of bed to race down to the
guardroom to carry out my guard duty. The problem
was that I had struck a deal with a notorious
character in the regiment to do my duty for me
that day, as he needed a bit of extra cash (soldiers
often made deals like this when they needed extra
money if theirs had run out before the end of the
month). I thought I was doing the Good Samaritan
deed by providing this soldier with the going rate
for a Saturday duty, and I had looked forward to my
Saturday free from guard duty. That was until the big
corporal shook me out of bed, informing me that this
soldier had not turned up for the duty and I would
have to now jump in and do it!

That particular Saturday was the coldest of the
year in Germany. I had to carry out the twenty-four-
hour duty on a normal two-hours-on/two-hours-off
routine, all the while watching my friends walk out
the gate towards the town for pizza, Bratwurst and
chips. News came in during the day that the soldier
who was supposed to do my duty had just carried on
drinking from the night before and was still drunk in

the town: drunk on the money I had given him for the duty. I was not in a particularly forgiving mood and I was freezing walking around the camp as a guard. The real challenge, of course, was what I was going to do about this: How would I react? Almost everyone told me I should 'fill him in', do him some damage. I was the regimental welterweight boxing champion at the time and this soldier was not exactly Arnold Schwarzenegger, so physically I could do it. But I was a Christian, so this was not an option at all. The real challenge came after I explained to my friends that I could not go down the physical-revenge route and some of them offered to do it for me, so that I could walk away free in my conscience. Tempting as it was, I had to decline their offers of vengeance. I chose to stay away from the soldier for a few days until I had prayed it through and could genuinely forgive him. After those few days, I found him and told him I forgave him. He was very sheepish in his response, but after he realized I was serious, he became notably relieved. It was one of the most effective times of witness I had as a serving soldier in the regiment. That 'cooling off' period was, for me, a time when I had to pray to God that I would not be led into temptation. Had this soldier come through those gates at 3 a.m. when I was at my coldest (and probably at my angriest), it could have turned out very differently. God answered by giving me time to reflect and pray. He made sure I was not led into temptation.

## ASR Ken Surgenor

A non-Christian soldier whom I have got to know well has said to me time and time again that, when he does something wrong, he feels he must do something good or right to make up for his wrong-doing. I have explained to him that, yes, we are dust and flesh, but within each of us lives a precious eternal soul, created by God and precious enough that the Lord Jesus Christ took not only my sin but the sin of the world upon Himself, and suffered in my place upon a cross, in order that I might have my sins forgiven and be reconciled to God. Yet, having had my sins forgiven, I am still flesh and my natural inclination is to sin—and I will sin. The Bible reminds us again and again of our tendency to sin, and that our best line of defence is to guard our walk by putting on the whole armour of God and to keep our eyes on Jesus and the cross. I am reminded again and again that greater men than I have fallen from grace. We need to finish the course and finish it well for the prize of the kingdom to come through the power, and the glory of a sovereign God, for all eternity.

## ASR David Murray

When talking to some soldiers once, I explained to them that God is not to blame for all the wrong-doing in this world. I told them that God does not tempt us to sin; we are more than capable of sinning on our own. God is the opposite of sin, and He encourages us to be holy, as He is holy. I also explained to them that God exists and so does Satan: turning to God for help means getting protection from the evil one. The Christian is protected by spiritual armour. The unbeliever is without armour, so is exposed to every attack of temptation and sin. This really hit home with the soldiers!

### ASR Meg Atkinson

As I was sitting with a group of soldiers who came mainly from Commonwealth countries and who had had religious upbringings, I noticed that their talking and walking didn't match up. Challenging them on particular issues, I discovered why some were falling short. I shared with them that if we want to remain standing in the battle and withstand the enemy, we must, by faith, put on all the defensive armour of God, and this means daily spending time with the Lord. Some of the boys thought they had the resources to beat the enemy's temptations, so I reminded them that our struggle is not against flesh and blood, but against the rulers of darkness and the spiritual forces of evil. All agreed that to be delivered we need to be daily in touch with the Deliverer.

The Soldiers' and Airmen's Scripture Readers Association's (SASRA) chief objective is to befriend Soldiers and Airmen and introduce them to the Good News of the Lord Jesus Christ. SASRA's opportunity "behind the wire", is unique, and we would be delighted if you would join us in this mission.

SASRA can send free materials to you that will give you a better understanding of the work. We are blessed by many who are faithful in prayer; and SASRA's Prayer Bulletins, Ready Magazines and Regional Reports will equip you to intercede and advocate for the work, within a local church context. To sign up please visit our website at sasra.org.uk and click on the tab marked "Support Us". You can also receive Facebook updates about SASRA's newest events by going to facebook.com/sasra.org.uk.

Since 1838 SASRA has known the gracious supply of the Lord for all its needs. SASRA receives no financial support from the public purse. Indeed, the work continues only because of generous financial support from the Lord's people.

If you would like to make a gift, set up a standing order or receive information about making a gift in your will, please use the website address above or contact SASRA on 03000 301 302 and ask for the Finance Director.

Matthew 24:44 (ESV) records, "Therefore you also must be ready, for the Son of Man is coming at an hour you do not expect." Please join SASRA's mission and give our military personnel every opportunity to be ready. They make profound sacrifices for us; will you do the same for them?

# Yes I want to HELP PARTNER with SASRA's ministry.

☐ **A ONE-OFF GIFT**

☐ **£10 can buy a hard-wearing Bible for a soldier or airman.**

☐ **£50 can fund a Scripture Reader taking the gospel to soldiers/airmen on exercise.**

☐ **£100 can pay for a whole Bible study course.**

☐ **£ _____ (please fill in the amount of your choice)**
**I enclose my (cash/cheque) donation to sponsor SASRA's work.**

☐ **I do not wish to receive an acknowledgement.**

Or if you wish to donate using your credit/debit card please either visit the donate page on the SASRA website **www.sasra.org.uk** or alternatively telephone SASRA HQ on **03000 301302**

☐ **REGULAR GIFT to support the work of SASRA**

**STANDING ORDER**

To _____ Bank PLC _____ Branch _____ Sort Code

Please pay to the account of SASRA, sorting code 161926 account number 10139767 the sum of

£ _____ ☐ each month ☐ quarter ☐ half year ☐ annually from my

account number ☐☐☐☐☐☐☐☐

Starting on ☐☐ / ☐☐ until further notice.

Signature: _____ Date: _____

**Boost your donation by 25p of Gift Aid for every £1 you donate**

Gift Aid is claimed by the charity from the tax you pay for the current tax year. Your address is needed to identify you as a current UK taxpayer. In order to Gift Aid your donation you must tick the box below.

☐ I want to Gift Aid my donation of £ _____ and any donation I make in the future or have made in the past 4 years to the Soldiers' and Airmen's Scripture Readers Association.

I am a UK taxpayer and understand that if I pay less Income Tax and/or Capital Gains Tax than the amount of Gift Aid claimed on all my donations in that tax year it is my responsibility to pay any difference. I will notify SASRA if I wish to cancel this declaration, change my name or address or no longer pay sufficient tax on my income or capital gains.

Signature: _____ Date: _____

**(PLEASE RETURN TO SASRA HQ)**

Name Mr/Mrs/Ms/Other _____

Address _____

_____ Postcode: _____

Email _____

We will hold the information you give us for administrative purposes. If you do not wish to receive any further news from us please write to: Supporter Services at our address. We never pass on contact details to any other organisation.

**SASRA** Havelock House, Barrack Road, Aldershot, Hampshire GU11 3NP
Telephone: **03000 301302** email: **admin@sasra.org.uk**

**www.sasra.org.uk**

Registered Charity No 235708 In Scotland SCO 39130